THE COMPARATIVE STUDY OF

FOREIGN POLICY

Volume 4, Sage Library of Social Research

SAGE LIBRARY OF SOCIAL RESEARCH

Also in this series:

The Comparative Study of Foreign Policy

A Survey of Scientific Findings

Patrick J. McGowan
Howard B. Shapiro

Volume 4
SAGE LIBRARY OF
SOCIAL RESEARCH

 SAGE PUBLICATIONS   Beverly Hills   London

For information address:

SAGE PUBLICATIONS, INC.
275 South Beverly Drive
Beverly Hills, California 90212

SAGE PUBLICATIONS LTD
St George's House / 44 Hatton Garden
London EC1N 8ER

Printed in the United States of America

International Standard Book Number 0-8039-0258-1(C)
0-8039-0207-7(P)

Library of Congress Catalog Card No. 72-98040

FIRST PRINTING

To Our Families

PREFACE

This brief book represents an attempt to survey and to integrate within a single framework current knowledge about the foreign policy behavior of nation states. It is therefore distinct from the usual propositional inventory in that we deal only with documented findings and not with propositions asserting cause and effect relations that are unsupported by systematic evidence. Our model in this enterprise has been the work of Bernard Berelson and Gary A. Steiner, whose *Human Behavior: An Inventory of Scientific Findings* (New York: Harcourt, Brace and World, 1964), has demonstrated both the scholarly and pedagogical usefulness of such surveys.

Our primary debt incurred in the writing of this book is to the scholars who have been venturesome enough to view foreign policy as a form of human behavior that is open to scientific investigation. It is their growing body of work that suggested the need for this book and which enabled us to write it. We hope that we have done justice to their achievements. In addition, many of these scholars were kind enough to bring to our attention relevant articles and books which we had omitted from earlier drafts. To name each would create a list almost as long as our bibliography. We trust that a collective "thank you" is sufficient! We also found particularly helpful the comments of an anonymous reviewer associated with Yale University Press, and we hope that this final version of our work meets his well-taken criticisms.

We would also like to acknowledge our debt to several colleagues within Syracuse University's International Relations Program. Its Director, Professor William D. Coplin, provided intellectual and material encouragement that greatly aided in the completion of our work. Professor Michael K. O'Leary read an earlier draft and used it in some of his classes which provided a useful source of critical suggestions. The Program and the Department of Political Science both create a stimulating atmosphere in which one can get on with one's work without being nagged by trivialities. McGowan would also like to thank Syracuse University for a semester's leave during which the finishing touches were made on the manuscript. Our typists, Mrs. Dorothy Bramhall, Mrs. Gloria Katz and Mrs. Sally La Mar, were patient and always efficient co-workers.

Finally, we would like to thank our readers in advance. We appreciate your spending time in reading this book and we hope that you will help us improve it by writing to us about articles, mongraphs, and books that should be included in future editions of this *Survey*. In this fashion we can collectively build a firmer foundation for the comparative study of foreign policy, which is why we wrote this book in the first place.

—P.J.M
—H.B.S.

TABLE OF CONTENTS

About the Authors

PATRICK J. McGOWAN is an assistant professor of political science at the Maxwell School, Syracuse University, a member of its program of International Relations and Director of its program of Eastern African Studies. He received his M.A. degree from the School of Advanced International Studies, Johns Hopkins University; his Ph.D. in political science was awarded by Northwestern University in 1970. Professor McGowan is editor of the *Sage International Yearbook of Foreign Policy Studies* and a member of the editorial board of the *American Journal of Political Science*. His publications include *American Foreign Policy: An Introduction to Analysis and Evaluation* (with William D. Coplin and Michael K. O'Leary; Duxbury); chapters in *Comparing Foreign Policies: Theories, Findings, Methods* (James N. Rosenau, ed.; Sage Publications); as well as articles in the *Journal of Asian and African Studies* and *International Studies Quarterly*. His current research focuses on a comparison of the foreign policy behavior of 32 African states, studies of political leadership and elites in Eastern Africa, and the methodology of comparative and international political research.

HOWARD SHAPIRO received his Ph.D. in political science (1973) from the Maxwell School, Syracuse University, where he is currently a research associate in the International Relations Program. Primarily interested in international politics and foreign policy, he is the co-author of *Introductory Case Studies for International Relations: Vietnam, the Middle East, and the Environmental Crisis;* the co-author of a chapter in *The Simulation of Intersocietal Relations*

(Joseph D. Ben-Dak, ed.); and the author of a chapter in *American Foreign Policy: An Introduction to Analysis and Evaluation.* His current research focuses on the application of social psychological concepts to foreign policy positions and on the general question of the resolution of international issues, with particular attention to the link between domestic politics and international politics.

Chapter I

INTRODUCTION

The goal of any discipline which claims the title of "science" must be to develop a body of theoretically organized knowledge that is based on cumulative empirical research. In spite of the enormous increase in the number of empirical investigations conducted in recent years, there is little of a cumulative nature in foreign policy studies. A handful of scholars have employed the findings of others in their research; but for the most part, scholars have not attempted to verify, incorporate, or build upon the work of others.

This *Survey* is designed to help develop cumulative knowledge in one of the fields of international relations and political science: the comparative study of foreign policy. This is a relatively new subject, but it already has a substantial empirical literature. It is our hope that, by bringing together the findings of this literature, we can help to impart some order to the field while it is still in its early stages and show scholars and students what works can form the basis of further investigations.

Our book is related to the goal of cumulative knowledge in four separate ways. First, it can be of help in the necessary process of replication of research. Scholars will be able to see what works have been replicated, in what manner and with what result, and whether there is a need for further replication. They will also be able to compare works that, though not replications, are similar to, and modify, other research. And, in those many instances where replication has not been attempted, they will be able to decide which studies are worthy of further investigation.

Second, as we shall demonstrate in this *Survey*, there are many areas of research that remain unexamined. For example, hardly any work has been done on the relationships between characteristics of foreign policy elites—a subclass of the political elite—and foreign policy behavior. In a similar fashion, most research has been cross-sectional; consequently, there are very few findings produced by comparative research on the behavior of nations over time. Before we can be cumulative, we must initiate research into *every* aspect of foreign policy behavior; and this volume identifies a number of topics that are still to be studied for the first time in a comparative fashion.

Third, the *Survey* can be used in the construction of "pre-theories" or working hypotheses about the causes and effects of foreign policy behavior.[1] While only a few studies have been concerned with determining the relative potency of independent variables, the studies of different authors can be compared with this object in mind. For example, if one study finds only a weak relationship between independent variable X_1 and dependent variable Y under certain conditions, and a study by a different author finds a strong relationship between independent variable X_2 and dependent variable Y under similar conditions, then we have established relative potency, although it may be only of a crude sort because particular aspects of the research may not be identical.

Fourth, this *Survey* can be of use in developing cumulative knowledge because it helps to relate scientific findings to theory. Instead of merely reporting the findings of research, it synthesizes these findings into general statements or propositions. These propositional statements, while certainly not expressions of "general theory," are not the specific findings of research either. They are general hypothetical statements whose variable concepts are in theoretical and not in operational form.[2] Throughout the *Survey*, the term "proposition" will be reserved for these general statements, while the term "finding" will refer to the specific results of a researcher's study.

Finally, although this point is not directly related to the goal of cumulative knowledge, it should be noted that the *Survey* can be used in college level courses on comparative foreign policy and international relations.[3] It provides a concise and organized overview of the "state of the field"— the kinds of questions considered, the methodologies and techniques employed, and the substantive results of research. Thus, the student may find the *Survey* useful in choosing an area of research that interests him and in rather painlessly mastering an already large literature on foreign policy.

A Note on Scientific Methods in the Study of Foreign Policy

This book is not the place to develop an extended argument defending the usefulness of a scientific approach to foreign policy studies. We take this for granted and we think that the research surveyed herein demonstrates the soundness of our viewpoint.[4] Nor can we provide in this *Survey* an exposition of scientific methods as applied to the study of social behavior. In any case there are already a large number of sound monographs that have been written with just this objective in mind.[5] Rather, we shall limit ourselves to a discussion of those aspects of methodology and research techniques that are germane to the scope and objectives of this *Survey*. In brief, these are: the nature of concepts, the problems of concept formation, and the operationalization or measurement of concepts; the nature of theory and generalizations; and the application of bivariate and multivariate statistical routines to the description of empirical findings. Important as these topics undoubtably are, they form only a part of what is normally treated in methodological discussions.

There is no need to fear methodology, for it is all rather simple, except when put in the hands of philosophers of science; then it becomes most difficult indeed! Every discipline has a set of procedures and rules that it uses to produce findings and to communicate them to other members of the profession—chemists do it, biologists do it, anthropologists do it, and so do political scientists. Methodology is what permits researchers to make theoretical claims about the causes and consequences of foreign policy, to verify these claims by looking at the real world, and then to communicate what has been learned to other interested scholars. Thus, methods represent the behavior of scientists. This behavior relies heavily on logic, for scientists do not like to be illogical since experience shows that mistakes usually follow. Methodology is not the use of particular research techniques like statistics or computers. Methodology provides rules that have proven over time to be useful for making public the scientist's private understanding of how the world works.

Philosophers of science help when they explicate the logic of what scientists actually do and when they lay down rules to follow if one wants to maximize clarity, precision, and one's ability to communicate to other minds; but that is all they do. We cannot stress too much that methodology is behavior. It is what scientists do in making theories, trying to verify them, and then openly communicating their results to each other.

Particularly useful to scientists are concepts. In research we do not deal with every specific event and object; rather, students of foreign policy seek general knowledge. Concepts are words used to designate classes of objects and events. Thus, in foreign policy studies we speak of "threats," "conflict," and "nationalism" which are types of actions or events and of "size," "development" and "political accountability" which are characteristics of certain objects: nation-states. The researcher has an idea or conception of something he suspects is important to the understanding of foreign policy behavior. He then defines the idea by saying that it means such and such and that it will be represented by the following term or symbol.

Thus, it may be that countries differ in their foreign policy behavior because they are more or less internally unified. States that are unified culturally, like France, might have consistent foreign policies, while states like Nigeria that combine a variety of religious, linguistic, and social groupings might have inconsistent foreign policies. We can then use the term "cultural pluralism" to mean our conception of variation in the value uniformity of countries. Our symbol, cultural pluralism, *means* our conception. Cultural pluralism *designates* certain characteristics of national societies. These characteristics of societies are *included in* our conception of value uniformity. These relationships are represented in Figure 1.

This example of cultural pluralism illustrates a number of important points about concepts and conceptual definitions.

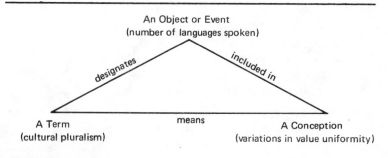

SOURCE: After Zetterberg, op. cit., p. 32.

Figure 1: THE PROCESS OF CONCEPTUAL DEFINITION

To use concepts we must first make use of some language— either English or some symbolic language like formal logic or mathematics. Concepts are represented by terms or symbols in these languages. We use a selected symbol like pluralism to designate a set of empirical phenomena: national variations in language, religion, values and so on. It makes no sense to say our definition of cultural pluralism is true or false. We have stipulated what we mean by the term, and that is all there is to it. Our definitions can be criticized if they are vague or if they are ambiguous, but not on the grounds that they are false. Scientific concepts do not try to capture the "essence" of some phenomenon; they merely state that, "Henceforth in this discussion, when we say 'cultural pluralism,' we shall be referring to the following set of features of national societies . . .".

Useful concepts can also be distinguished on grounds in addition to their clarity of definition. First, any concept of use to a scientist must have some empirical referent—it must relate to something in the world. If we cannot identify objects and events that are instances of cultural pluralism and consistent foreign policy, then we cannot use such concepts in research. But, while all scientific concepts must have empirical referents, these can be direct or indirect. Thus, "dictatorship" and "cultural pluralism" cannot be directly observed but must be defined in terms of lower-order concepts concerning the extent of civil liberties or the number of languages spoken, for example. Indirectly observable concepts like these are often called *postulational concepts*. Directly observable concepts are called *concrete concepts;* an instance would be "population," which can be determined by counting if necessary.

The second criterion of scientific usefulness of concepts is their theoretical significance. Concepts like "cultural pluralism" are defined because it is thought that they are related to other important concepts like "consistency" in foreign policy behavior. If research demonstrates that as pluralism declines, consistency of foreign policy increases, then the concept of cultural pluralism will enter the scientific vocabulary of foreign policy researchers and be accepted as a useful concept. The concepts elaborated in the framework of Chapter II are suggested as useful for organizing the findings of research and for suggesting further research. This is an instance of theoretical significance, although the framework is not a theory, as we shall see.

Postulational and concrete concepts represent *empirical concepts,* and all concepts that are found in the subjects and predicates of scientific statements are of this type. A second type of concept is also used in research. These are *relational concepts* that link empirical concepts in statements. Thus, "the greater" the cultural pluralism, "the less" consistent the foreign policy of nation states. Other instances of relational concepts are "and," "or," "if . . . then," "+" and "—." These concepts are essential in linking empirical concepts in hypotheses and in generalizations. They represent logical categories and mathematical operations and therefore have no empirical content themselves. But, along with empirical concepts, relational concepts are the building blocks of scientific statements.

The final aspect of concepts that we must discuss is the problem of operationalization. Empirical concepts, either directly or indirectly, must be linked to observable objects or events. This is what one does when one operationalizes a concept. Thus, whereas *conceptually* cultural pluralism refers to the degree of variation in the value patterns within a society, *operationally* we can measure cultural pluralism by constructing an index based on the number of languages spoken in a country. The more languages spoken, the greater the pluralism. Such a measurement operation is necessary if we are ever going to see if pluralism is related to consistency of foreign policy, as we expect.

The comparative study of foreign policy is in its early stages. As a result of this situation there is disagreement on the important concepts to use in research. We do not know what are the basic types of foreign policy, nor do we know the attributes of nations and their leaders that are likely to be related to foreign policy behavior. Thus, each researcher tends to use his pet concepts, defined in his own way, and operationalized differently from previous work. Eventually, some agreement must emerge from this conceptual chaos. This *Survey* can aid in this process by demonstrating the variety of concepts currently used and by identifying the ones that appear related to important aspects of foreign policy behavior.

Although there is no agreement in the field of the comparative study of foreign policy about the key concepts, no one would say that there are not a large number of them available for use by researchers. At the same time, one would be hard-pressed to say that there is any theory in the field. "Theory" can be defined as a set of deductively related generalizations, of which we shall say more presently. What is striking about the social sciences, including foreign policy studies, is the absence of generally agreed-upon theories. Theories are answers to "why" questions. For example: "Why does extensive cultural pluralism lead to an inconsistent foreign policy?" An answer to such a question would be a theory or, at least, part of a theory. It is unlikely, however, that if you asked a group of specialists in foreign policy studies why anything is the way it is, you would get consistent theoretical answers. Let us look at this issue more closely.

To make theories, just as we do when we define concepts, we must make use of language—either natural language or a formal language. Thus, the basic parts of any theory are statements, such as "Cultural pluralism is negatively related to consistency in foreign policy." In such a statement, we recognize two empirical concepts ("cultural pluralism" and "foreign policy consistency") and one relational concept ("is negatively related"). Thus, we state that as cultural pluralism goes up, consistency goes down. Since this statement uses empirical or synthetic concepts, it is called a *synthetic statement*. Synthetic statements that are parts of theories come in two types. If they have not yet been checked against data and shown to be correct, they are called "hypotheses." Our statement concerning cultural pluralism is really an hypothesis for there has not been any systematic research to test its truth content. For statements to be acceptable hypotheses in scientific work, they must be open to checking to see if they are true or false. If a scientist cannot figure out a way to test a statement to see if it is false, then he will tend not to regard it as an hypothesis. If several "probes" of the hypothesis in different research projects have shown the hypothesis to be accurate, it then becomes a "generalization" that has been validated against evidence that could have shown it to be false. The synthetic statements we find in theories are therefore either validated generalizations or as yet untested hypotheses.

A second type of statement is found in theories. There are *analytical statements* which, as their name suggests, cannot be called true or false. Analytical statements offer definitions and they are vital, for we must obviously know what is the subject matter of our theory. However, they do not add anything to our empirical knowledge, as we have seen in discussing concept definition. Rather, they merely lay down rules for the use of words in the context of the theory we are studying.

The "propositions" presented in this *Survey* for the most part are midway between being hypotheses and generalizations. There has in every case been at least one study that has demonstrated their correctness, so they are not untested hypotheses. On the other hand, except perhaps in the area of the relation between domestic conflict and foreign conflict behavior (see Chapter VI), there have not been sufficient replications and independent tests to say they represent firm, well-established generalizations. We need more replications and independent tests of hypotheses in the field of foreign policy studies so that we can have sufficient confidence in our findings to say that they have established some useful generalizations.

This introduces an important methodological point. Since, in the end, scientific methods always rely on empirical evidence, it is possible that the next time we test what appears to be a well-established relationship we will find it does not hold. This is clearly a logical possibility. Because every swan I have ever seen is white does not rule out the empirical possibility that black swans exist, as Europeans found out upon first visiting Australia. Thus, in science there is no final or absolute certainty or truth. All our knowledge is contingent upon the results of future research which may lead to its modification. Although recognition of this fact sometimes disillusions sophomores, it is in reality a cause for rejoicing. First, it gives us all a chance to make a contribution since there are no final answers in science. More profoundly, it means that science has a unique self-corrective mechanism built into it. While absolute truth can never be reached, the constant testing, modification, and reformulation of our theories—made possible because of the open and communicable methods of science—leads to ever more certain knowledge about why things are the way they are. Thus, this *Survey* presents some very plausible hypotheses that have just not been supported by evidence and other less obvious relationships that, up to this point, have been found to be true.

Generalizations or, as they are sometimes called, scientific laws, are very important because, as we have said, theories are sets of generalizations that are deductively related. Laws come in two forms: universal and statistical. A *universal generalization* is in the form "all X are Y"—like "all men are mortal." *Statistical generalizations* come in the form "some X are Y"—like "98% of Swedes are Protestants." Most generalizations in the social sciences are statistical in form, but they are, nevertheless, highly useful. Thus, we know that foreign policy activity is related to the size and wealth of states. The larger and wealthier a country, the more foreign policy activity it undertakes. This represents a rather well-confirmed statistical generalization in foreign policy studies.

As it stands, alone by itself, it is not a theory; it is just an isolated generalization. However, if we could relate it to other generalizations from which it could be deduced, then we would have a theory about the causes of activity levels in foreign affairs. We want to know why it is true that the larger and wealthier a country is, the more active is its foreign policy. Our answer will be a theory. We might demonstrate that it is empirically true that size and wealth create a need to interact with the foreign environment to protect extensive frontiers and to enhance wealth by trade. If we combine this "need" hypothesis with the assumption that, all other things being equal, statesmen will act in foreign affairs to meet the needs of their society, we have a deductively organized theory of the level of foreign policy activity of states.

What does our theory contain? First, there is an untested assumption about how decision-makers behave. Every deductive theory will have a set of such axioms or assumptions that in the context of the particular theory are taken as given. But, if our assumption about statesmen always trying to meet the needs of their societies leads to fruitful predictions, we will increasingly come to believe that it is a reasonable assumption to make about this aspect of human behavior. You should also note that in any theory of foreign policy there must be either assumptions or generalizations about human behavior, for in the end that is what foreign policy is all about. Also, note that we assumed that this rule of decision-making behavior held only when all other things were equal. This is the often used condition of *ceteris paribus*. Some sort of assumption about the conditions under which a theory will hold must always be made, and the *ceteris paribus* assumption is the most common starting place in science. Besides our assumption, we have a broad generalization that the size and wealth of states is positively related to a need to interact with the environment. From this assumption and the need generalization, we can deduce the generalization that the larger and the wealthier a state, the greater its foreign policy activity.

A theory in which a set of generalizations are deductively related is hierarchical in form. Beginning with a few axiomatic assumptions and the rules of logic, one can deduce theorems, many of which are then either untested hypotheses or confirmed generalizations. There are not many theories of this type in the social sciences and particularly in foreign policy studies, but it is the goal of any scientific approach to develop such theories. At this stage of development in foreign policy studies, it is more frequent to encounter "factor theories" of foreign policy behavior. These are not organized in a hierarchical fashion, but rather like the spokes of a wheel. Consistency of foreign policy is seen to be caused by a low level of cultural pluralism and by several other factors like, perhaps, the experience of the statesmen in foreign affairs and the degree of threat that confronts the acting state. Such a theory can be expressed as an equation in the form Y = A + B + C, and it has the structure illustrated in Figure 2.

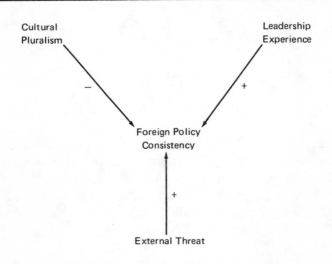

Figure 2: THE STRUCTURE OF A FACTOR THEORY

How are theories generated? They arise from the interaction of the scientist and his data. A relationship between two concepts is expected to exist. An hypothesis is stated to represent this relationship. Reasons why the hypothesis might be true are stated in the form of higher-level generalizations and assumptions. The researcher then examines a set of appropriate data to see if the hypothesis is supported or falisified by the data. Does the relationship indeed hold as expected? The methods used to test hypotheses derive from the work of John Stuart Mill. In his *A System of Logic,* Mill developed four methods and five "canons" of reasoning from them to permit the scientist to make inferences from data to the truth or falsity of his hypotheses. The clearest presentation we know of these methods is presented by Copi, but Graham also discusses them.[6]

We cannot present an analysis here of Mill's methods. What is important to note is that they rely on *comparative analysis.* Each of his methods for making inferences about hypotheses uses several instances of the phenomenon in question. In no case can the hypothesis be tested by looking at only one instance of the thing in question. This is why the comparative study of foreign policy and the scientific study of foreign policy are synonymous. Scientific method uses comparison very heavily whenever hypotheses are checked against data; and since all sciences are empirical at some point, they all use comparison.

What are the purposes of theory? Theories must be important, for scientists certainly spend a great deal of time talking about them. The main purpose of theory is to explain why things are the way they are. Our example concerning the level of foreign policy activity illustrates this. Every theory will explain phenomena; most theories also permit one to make predictions, since explanation and prediction are two sides of the same coin. Explanations look backwards. They answer the question, "Why did this happen?" Predictions look forward. They state when this will happen again.

Clearly, if one has a good explanation of why something is the way it is, then one can predict that when the conditions which caused the phenomenon in the past are again present, it will happen again. This leads to a final important point about theory.

If you can successfully explain and predict some phenomenon like war, then you can control it. Unfortunately, we do not have theories of foreign policy conflict and war that permit us both to explain and to predict its occurrence. If we did, then we would be in a position perhaps to manipulate those variables that have been shown to lead to war in such a way as to cause them to lead to peace. This is why theory is so important from a practical point of view. If you do not like big powers intervening in the affairs of small countries, such as those of Southeast Asia, you need a theory of intervention in foreign affairs before you can have any chance of ending what you don't like, or of producing what you do like.

Finally, besides types of theory such as hierarchical and factor, levels of theory are often distinguished. How broad is the set of phenomena explained by the theory? If it is broad, covering all forms of foreign policy behavior, this would then be called a "general theory" of foreign policy. If the theory explained selected aspects of foreign policy, like foreign aid behavior or war, then it would be a "middle-range theory." Finally, if one had established a relationship between cultural pluralism and consistency of foreign policy or about size and wealth leading to activity in foreign policy, one would have isolated "generalizations." These three levels of theory are illustrated in Figure 3.

Any field of scientific inquiry can be evaluated by the extent to which it has a general theory that encompasses middle-range theories and a host of generalizations. From this point of view, the comparative study of foreign policy is not yet a well-developed science. What we have is a number of generalizations, many of which are unrelated and only partially validated. There are a few middle-range theories and

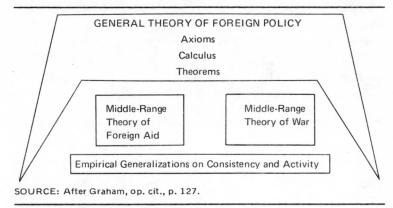

SOURCE: After Graham, op. cit., p. 127.

Figure 3: IDEAL RELATIONSHIP OF LEVELS OF THEORY

no general theory at all. However, the paucity of middle-range theories and the lack of general theory is not proof that such are impossible in the study of foreign policy. If one adopts a scientific attitude toward the study of foreign policy, as we have in this book, then one must continually strive to interrelate generalizations into middle-range theories in the hope that as knowledge advances, general theory will eventually be possible to state. We think this *Survey* will prove helpful in this direction, for we have largely reported findings and propositions that, as we have said, are midway between hypotheses and generalizations. We have not tried to interrelate these propositions into middle-range theories. Such would be a useful activity for readers of this book. We certainly intend to try this in our own future work.

We shall conclude this methodological note by discussing the technical problems of measurement and statistical analysis in foreign policy studies very briefly. As we have already mentioned, concepts must be operationalized if empirical research is to be done on expected relationships. When concepts are viewed from the point of view of measurement, they are usually called "variable concepts" or just "variables," for short. If a researcher has a clear idea of the meaning of his concept, then he should have no trouble measuring it.

Four levels of measurement are usually distinguished in discussions of this topic. The simplest level is that of a "nominal scale," where classes or categories are established on the basis of "either . . . or" reasoning. Either this country is at war, or it is not at war. The answer will depend on our definition of the concept "war." Countries can then be sorted into classes of "at war" and "not at war." We have then "measured" this variable in a crude fashion. We could then proceed to divide countries into those that have capitalist economies and those that have socialist economies in the same way. Then, by making a two-by-two table, we would be able to see the relationship between being at war and type of economy, as illustrated in Table 1. Since a nominal scale is a form of measurement—"qualitative measurement"—we have indeed operationalized our concepts of being at war and type of economy. Thus, if one has a clear idea of what one is studying, *it is always possible to measure it.* And, since there are statistics like phi and chi square which are designed to establish the strength and likelihood of the distribution of cases in Table 1, we can always apply statistical techniques, *if we want to,* to the study of foreign policy phenomena.

The second level of measurement is ordinal, based upon

TABLE 1

HYPOTHETICAL DATA ON THE RELATIONSHIP OF ECONOMIC ORGANIZATION TO WARFARE (n=50 countries)

		INDEPENDENT VARIABLE		
		Capitalist Economy	Socialist Economy	
DEPENDENT VARIABLE	At War	10	5	15
	Not at War	30	5	35
		40	10	50

"more-or-less" reasoning. "Ordinal scales" produce rank orders of the phenomenon in question. Thus, countries can be ranked as great powers, middle powers, small powers, and mini powers. Such a ranking, based upon explicit and objective criteria, can then be compared to other rankings, like participation in alliances, to inquire if "power magnitude" is related to "alliance membership." Rank orders are also a form of qualitative measurement; but again appropriate statistical techniques, such as Spearman's rho, have been developed to determine the degree of association between ordinal scales.

The two levels of measurement that are properly quantitative are "interval scales" and "ratio scales." A thermometer is an example of an interval scale that we use every day. The zero point is arbitrary, but the scale points are of equal intervals; hence the name. Thus, the difference between 60 degrees and 70 degrees is the same as the difference between 40 degrees and 50 degrees. The "population" of a country or its "wealth as measured by GNP per capita" are interval scales, because countries without population and some wealth could not exist. Ratio scales have true zero points, so that "the number of wars a country has fought since 1945" is a ratio scale because it is possible that a country's position could be zero on that scale. Powerful statistical techniques exist for studying interval and ratio scales, and researchers usually prefer, if possible, to work with either of these truly quantitative levels of measurement.

A frequently used technique, and one that many of the findings reported in this *Survey* are based upon, is "regression and correlation analysis" as applied to ratio and interval scales. The basic approach of regression analysis is to fit a line to a scatter of points plotted in two-dimensional space, as illustrated in Figure 4. Since one is fitting a straight line, it has the form $Y = a + bX$. What is important for this discussion is the *regression coefficient:* b. This represents the degree to which changes in X lead to changes in Y. The sign of b is important in this respect. For line A of Figure 4, the relationship is direct or positive; and as X increases, so does Y. In this case b would be positive. In the case of line B in the figure, the relationship is negative, or inverse; as X increases, Y decreases. Here b is negative in sign. Thus, the regression coefficient tells us some very useful information about the nature of the relationship between two variable concepts. It shows first of all the direction of the relationship; and second, it tells us how the dependent variable, Y, changes in response to a unit change in the independent variable, X.

Regression analysis per se does not tell us how strong the relationship is between the two variables, although this can be figured from a regression analysis. More usual, however, is to calculate the *correlation coefficient* or r, which is a measure of the ratio of explained and unexplained variation in Y. If all points in the figure were exactly on lines A and B, then r would be + 1.0 in the case of A, and −1.0 in the case of B. When r = 0.0, there is no relationship between the variables. In doing statistical analysis on computers, already prepared programs will print out scatter plots like Fig. 4 and give both b and r as a matter of course.

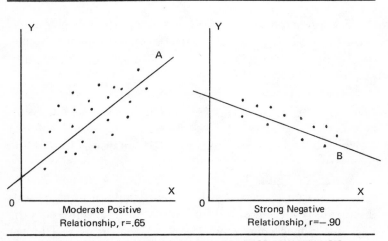

Moderate Positive
Relationship, r=.65

Strong Negative
Relationship, r=−.90

Figure 4: ASPECTS OF CORRELATION AND REGRESSION ANALYSIS

Besides knowing the strength and direction of a relationship, the researcher wants to know the likelihood of observing such a relationship by chance. Chance, and not the truth of the hypothesis under investigation, is always a possible reason for observing a given relationship. Researchers thus usually make "tests of significance" to check the counter-hypothesis that chance has produced these results. Obviously, they hope that they can reject the hypothesis of chance association in favor of their original causal hypothesis. However, since the procedures used are open and replicable, it is difficult to cheat on such tests, which is one of their major advantages.

Thus, statistics are used to examine the validity of hypothetical relationships between variables. The application of statistical analysis, whatever the level of measurement (for there are appropriate techniques at the nominal up to the ratio level), provides information about the direction, strength, and likelihood of the observed relationships. Such information is vital for transforming plausible hypotheses into confirmed generalizations. Throughout this *Survey* you will encounter propositions that relate variables in this fashion. Where possible, we have reported the strength and direction of the findings that support the propositions.

One final point deserves mention. In our explanation of statistical techniques, we have used bivariate examples. We have related just two variables at a time. However, the world is not that simple, and far more likely are factor theory explanations that relate a dependent variable to several independent variables in the form of equations like $Y = a + b_1 A + b_2 B + b_3 C$. This is multivariate analysis—as when Y equals consistency of foreign policy and A, B, and C represent, respectively: cultural pluralism, statesmen's experience, and foreign threats. Unfortunately, most of the research reported in this *Survey* is based upon bivariate rather than the more sophisticated and realistic multivariate analysis. Wherever possible, researchers in the comparative study of foreign policy must try to use more multivariate techniques so that we can, in fact, make all other things equal via the advanced statistical techniques of partial correlation and regression.[7]

These are only some of the topics that are studied in the methodology of the social sciences. Moreover, we have treated them in a very brief and an almost superficial manner. Our purpose has not been to make readers into competent methodologists, but rather to enhance the usefulness of this *Survey,* particularly for readers who were not previously familiar with this approach to foreign policy studies. If our discussion and the *Survey* itself lead you to think that there is something worthwhile in the comparative study of foreign policy, we will have achieved our aim. To be able to do comparative foreign policy research oneself would then mean reading the methodological and statistical works we have cited in this note and especially the empirical studies of foreign policy that are surveyed in this book.

NOTES

1. James N. Rosenau, "Pre-Theories and Theories of Foreign Policy," pp. 27-93 in R. B. Farrell (ed.) *Approaches to Comparative and International Politics* (Evanston, Ill.: Northwestern University Press, 1966).

2. Hubert M. Blalock, Jr., "The Measurement Problem: A Gap Between the Languages of Theory and Research," pp. 9-13 in H. M. Blalock, Jr. and A. Blalock (eds.) *Methodology in Social Research* (New York: McGraw-Hill, 1968).

3. A related teaching tool is the "Learning Package" by Patrick J. McGowan and Michael K. O'Leary in *Comparative Foreign Policy Analysis Materials* (Chicago: Markham, 1971).

4. An extended defense and application of this position is provided in, especially, Chapter 2 of James N. Rosenau, *The Scientific Study of Foreign Policy* (New York: Free Press, 1971).

5. We would recommend the following to the interested reader: G. J. Graham, Jr., *Methodological Foundations for Political Analysis* (Waltham, Mass.: Xerox, 1971); A. Kaplan, *The Conduct of Inquiry: Methodology for Behavioral Science* (San Francisco: Chandler, 1964); Patrick J. McGowan (ed.) *Comparative Political Analysis: A Reader in*

Metapolitics (New York: Dodd, Mead, forthcoming); W. G. Runciman, *Social Science and Political Theory* (Cambridge: Cambridge University Press, 1965); and H. L. Zetterberg, *On Theory and Verification in Sociology* (Totowa, N.J.: Bedminster, 1965).

6. See I. M. Copi, *An Introduction to Logic* (New York: Macmillan, 1953); and Graham, *op. cit.*, pp. 139-145.

7. The reader who wants to learn more about statistical techniques can consult the following books, which are listed in order of difficulty: L.C. Freeman, *Elementary Applied Statistics* (New York: John Wiley, 1965); H. M. Blalock, Jr., *Social Statistics* (New York: McGraw-Hill, 1960); and H. M. Blalock, Jr. (ed.) *Causal Models in the Social Sciences* (Chicago: Aldine-Atherton, 1971).

Chapter II

ORGANIZATION

Introduction

The first step in preparing this *Survey* was to obtain promising titles from several standard indexes[1] for the years 1955 to 1972 under such headings as foreign policy, international relations, diplomacy, war, United Nations, and comparative politics. References in books and articles were also a useful source of works, as were the suggestions of many colleagues. Several hundred works were then scanned, and about 200—all English language journal articles or books—were judged to represent empirical research in the comparative study of foreign policy.

These works had to meet several criteria in order to be included in the *Survey*. First, they had to be published; thus, we included doctoral dissertations, but not mimeographed papers presented to professional conferences. Second, they had to be empirical. In an effort not to be rigid, "empirical" was defined not as quantitative, but as an attempt at a controlled investigation. Thus, works using comparative case studies as well as those using quantitative data were included. Third, the research had to be comparative. It could examine either two or more actors, i.e., states or subunits of states, or two or more comparable instances of behavior of one or more actors. Finally, the works had to account for the causes and/or consequences of foreign policy behavior by relating two or more variables; thus, many studies developing a measure of one variable, though important to the development of the field, were not included.

Our decision to include only published works was made necessary by the impossibility of tracing down all of the occasional papers, drafts, conference papers and other writings that have yet to be sanctified by printer's ink. Important findings are not always published, however. We should mention, therefore, several ongoing research projects that have produced numerous papers, only some of which have been published. Our readers will be aware of these projects and can contact the individuals involved if they wish to read their numerous unpublished papers.

The longest standing project which has also produced the greatest number of published studies is the Dimensionality of Nations Project (DON) under the direction of Professor Rudolph J. Rummel of the University of Hawaii (see Rummel, 1972).[2] Based on 236 aggregate variables for over 80 nations in the mid-and late-1950s, DON aims to map the structural variations among nations and, within a "field theory," to analyze the interactions of these states. Works by Rummel, Tanter, Wilkenfeld, and others examined in our *Survey* have used the DON data. Numerous unpublished DON Reports are available, but were not surveyed for this book.

A second large-scale project which examines the interactions of all states is the World Event Interaction Survey (WEIS), under the direction of Professor Charles A. McClelland of the University of Southern California. This project aims to map the processes of interaction within the international system by coding "event interactions" between states and other international actors as reported in the prestige press of the world, starting with the daily New York *Times.* To date, over 20,000 event interactions have been coded for about 150 actors during the period January 1966 through the end of 1971. Studies using the WEIS data by McClelland and Hoggard (1969) and Kegley (1971) have been used in the preparation of this *Survey* since the WEIS project represents the major collection of foreign policy acts presently available for comparative research. The WEIS project is breifly described in McClelland and Hoggard (1969: 711-713) and in the numerous unpublished papers available from the project.

A third major data study, under the direction of Professor J. David Singer of the University of Michigan, is the Correlates of War project, summarized in Singer (1972). This project has already resulted in a large number of published papers by Professors Singer, Melvin Small, and Michael Wallace. Many other papers have been prepared, but have yet to be published. The Correlates of War project takes a clearly defined dependent variable, warfare, and measures its incidence and development over time since 1815. Data are also collected on attributes of the state-actors and the international system during the same period of time. The empirical and normative concerns of the project are to develop causal theories of the onset and termination of war (empirical) so that this aspect of foreign policy behavior might be open to control (normative).

A number of collaborative research projects and seminars have recently focused explicitly on the comparative study of foreign policy. The Inter-University Comparative Foreign Policy Project (ICFP), which groups scholars from various Canadian and American universities, has held a summer seminar and has prepared a joint volume tentatively entitled *Comparing Foreign Policies: Theories, Findings, and Methods* which will be published in 1973 or 1974 by Sage Publications. Under the informal leadership of Professor James N.

Rosenau of the University of Southern California, the ICFP's prime goal is the development of empirically grounded foreign policy theory. Over thirty unpublished conference papers are available.

Related to the activities of the ICFP is the Comparative Research on the Events of Nations project (CREON), under the joint direction of Professors Charles F. Hermann of Ohio State, Maurice A. East of the University of Kentucky, and Steven A. Salmore of Rutgers University. CREON has collected over 11,500 foreign policy acts by 32 states during the period 1959-1968. The CREON project began in 1970 and it has so far produced a number of unpublished papers. Chapters in the *Comparing Foreign Policies* volume to be edited by Rosenau will probably be the first published versions of CREON materials.

All of the above research projects involve comparisons of the action of states that are world wide in scope. Parallel and complementary research on the foreign policy behavior of states in certain regions of the world is also underway. Professor Edward E. Azar of the University of North Carolina has collected a set of foreign policy behavior data concerning the major actors in the Middle East in his Conflict and Cooperation research project.[3] Azar has also made important contributions to the methodology of events data research. Many as yet unpublished papers are available from his project.

Also concerning this region is the Middle East Conflict and Cooperation Analysis (MECCA) project of Professor Robert Burrowes of New York University and The American University in Beirut. Burrowes has collected domestic and foreign policy events for four years selected from the period 1951 to 1967 for the major actors in the Middle East. Besides being able to relate domestic to foreign behavior, Burrowes is able to engage in time-series analysis and to check on the validity and reliability of his data since he is using a variety of sources.[4] The first published results of this project are likely to appear in the forthcoming *Comparing Foreign Policies* volume.

A final comparative foreign policy project with a regional focus is McGowan's African Foreign Relations and International Conflict Analysis (AFRICA) project. Over 14,500 foreign policy acts of thirty-two Black African states have been collected on a daily basis between January 1964 and December 1966. The purpose of the AFRICA project is to relate foreign policy behavior to subsequent domestic instability like coups d'état. Data collection was completed in 1972 and studies of African foreign policy behavior have not yet appeared but a study of the reliability and validity of the data will appear in the Rosenau-edited *Comparing Foreign Policies* volume.

All of these projects ranging from DON to the AFRICA study share certain common features. Many internal memoranda and preliminary studies have been produced which can be of great interest to students of foreign policy but which for various reasons are unlikely to be published. They can usually be obtained from the offices of the project directors. Second, the data collected are in quantitative form on IBM cards or computer tapes and discs. These data are available to other scholars either directly from the projects themselves or indirectly via the services of the Inter-University Consortium for Political Research in Ann Arbor, Michigan, whose International Relations Data Archive serves as a depository and diffusion center for this type of data.

Two other related developments are also contributing to the growth of the comparative study of foreign policy. An International Events and Foreign Policy Study Group has been formed within the International Studies Association. Its newsletter, *Leads and Lags,* which is available from Professor Philip M. Burgess of Ohio State University, keeps interested scholars abreast of developments in this field. Second, two new publishing ventures will provide an outlet for the growing number of empirical and comparative studies that are being done. The first is a new journal to be called *International Interactions,* which will be edited by Edward Azar of North Carolina. The second is the *Sage International*

Yearbook of Foreign Policy Studies which McGowan is editing for Sage Publications. Both the new journal and the *Yearbook* are expected to appear in 1973 and to publish the type of literature surveyed in our book.

A Framework of Comparative Foreign Policy Analysis

In *Political Participation,* Lester Milbrath notes, "A Summary, to be really serviceable, must integrate discrete facts into a somewhat comprehensive whole; thus, some sort of theory is required."[5] In line with Milbrath's suggestion, the propositions reported in this *Survey* will be integrated by reference to a framework which suggests the independent variables relevant to foreign policy (the dependent variable), and the ways in which these independent variables are connected to outputs. The framework is given in Figure 5, and it deserves some comment.

For us, the dependent variable of foreign policy behavior encompasses identifiable acts undertaken by the official representatives of national societies or their agents in order to control the behavior of their counterparts in ways desired by the actors. These acts can include opinions or attitudes expressed, but they must be by the *official* representatives of the nation; in other words, public opinion about another nation or a foreign policy issue is not considered a foreign policy output. However, there are some acts not directly connected with officials which will be considered as foreign policy outputs. These are the transnational activities—mostly trade, but also flows of people, communications, and the like—that are to some extent the consequences of previous official decisions. Such activities are an important component of a nation's foreign policy.

As can be seen from the framework given in Figure 5, foreign policy output is accounted for by a set of independent variables, of which nine categories are attributes of the actor and two are attributes of the external environment of the actor. These variable types introduce an interdiscipli-

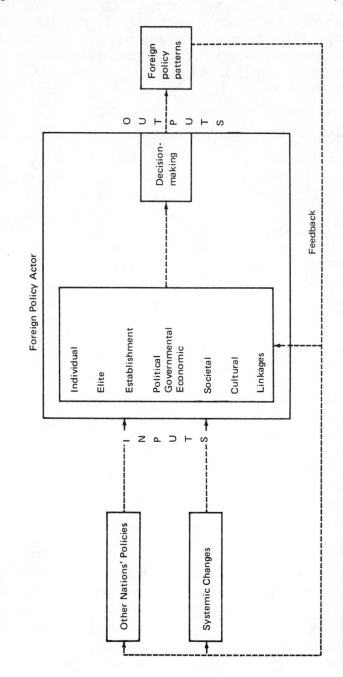

Figure 5: A FRAMEWORK FOR COMPARATIVE FOREIGN POLICY ANALYSIS

nary approach to the comparative study of foreign policy, for it is clear that the work of historians, economists, sociologists, anthropologists, psychologists, and political scientists will be necessary to understand their consequences for foreign policy.

Individual variables refer to the variable characteristics of identifiable persons who regularly make foreign policy for national societies (for example: prime ministers, presidents, party chairmen, and dictators). Characteristics of key decision-makers that are considered relevant are their personality traits, perceptions, beliefs, values, experiences, and social background attributes. This set of possible causal variables is distinct because it refers to what the leaders bring to the job as persons and not to the roles or institutional setting in which they make foreign policy. As we demonstrate in Chapter III, most research in comparative foreign policy on individual variables has focused on the *perceptions* of decision-makers and how this relates to their decision-making behavior and the policies they adopt. While perceptions are undoubtedly important, other aspects of individuals such as their personalities and social backgrounds are also worthy of study.

Elite variables relate to the aggregate characteristics of the country's foreign policy elite. In every state, foreign policy is made by a relatively small group of men and women. What is their average age and educational attainment? What proportion of this elite is civilian and what proportion is military? Most important, who are these elites, how did they get to be foreign policy elites, and how do they stay there? It may well be that foreign policy is made largely for the benefit of these elites, so that they can stay in power and enhance their status and self-esteem. There has not been much research of a comparative sort on the relationships between elite characteristics and their foreign policies. Obviously, until such research is undertaken, we cannot say whether or not this category of variables is useful in explaining the foreign policy behavior of nation states.

Establishment variables refer to the organizational features of a nation's foreign policy and national security departments. The studies surveyed in Chapter V have examined such establishment characteristics as the extent of conflict in the bureaucracy, its level of institutionalization, and the capabilities of the foreign affiars establishments of various nations. There is an extensive literature in the field of public administration, particularly in the area of organization theory, that may be relevant to explaining similarities and differences in foreign policy. This literature needs to be examined and establishment variables like the number, complexity, and institutionalization of these bureaucracies need to be related to patterns of foreign policy behavior. Of particular interest will be the patterns of conflict and competition among government agencies which seem so important to an understanding of American foreign policy. Comparative research has not yet established how general this phenomenon is in other countries.

Political variables group together attributes of the national political system such as the competitiveness of the party system, the level of political conflict and the activities of pressure groups in the foreign policy process. Political variables emphasize political processes within a country while *governmental* variables relate to structural attributes of the political system and nation as a whole, like its military capability, form of government, or date of independence. In Chapter VI we look at political variables like the accountability of the government to the people, the extent of domestic conflict in the political system and society (which has been extensively studied in relation to foreign conflict behavior), and the consequences of economic interest groups on foreign policies aiming toward greater integration among states. In Chapter VII governmental variables, like the form of government (presidential vs. parliamentary) and its military power, are examined. Comparative research on foreign policy behavior is perhaps richest in the area of political and governmental variables, as might be expected, since most of it has been done by political scientists. Yet, even here, we are only making a beginning and only in the area of the relationship between domestic and foreign conflict behavior has there developed a tradition of replication and cumulative inquiry.

Economic variables include factors that relate the economic structure and processes of a country to its foreign policies. Such features as the level of economic development, the amount and diversity of foreign trade, the balance of payments, and the rates of technological change and economic growth are all considered within this category. Marxian theory of foreign policy as elaborated by Lenin, Nkrumah and others places great stress on the determining nature of economic structure for foreign policy. "Imperialist" and "neo-colonial" foreign policies are asserted to be the consequence of "capitalist" economic organization. We view this as an empirical question in need of more research in the context of the comparative study of foreign policy.

Societal variables are aspects of the social structure, broadly defined, of national societies. This category includes such factors as size of population, population growth rates, social stratification patterns, and the degree of social modernization. Among the variables studied in a comparative framework that relate to societal characteristics are size and other features of population like its density and its rate of growth. This data is easily available, although often wildly inaccurate. Since sociologists have tended not to be concerned with foreign affairs, this area of research has been neglected—even though it would appear to relate to many aspects of foreign policy behavior, particularly via the key variable of modernization.

Cultural variables describe the cultural systems of national societies, such as their degree of cultural pluralism, patterns of national identity (degree of "nationalism"), and their information processing systems, the media. Russett (1967) has empirically identified five "sociocultural regions" that are likely to have distinct patterns of foreign policy behavior:

Afro-Asia, the Western Community, Latin America, the semi-developed Latins, and Eastern Europe. We have found that the major cultural variables so far used in comparative research have been ideology, race, and religion.

Linkage variables represent the historical traces of the actor's past foreign policy behavior. Traditions of past foreign economic and political involvement are likely to influence current and future behavior. Thus, all the past official actions of decision-makers and their agents as manifested in treaty ties, diplomatic representation, international organization memberships, and foreign aid are included in the linkage cluster of variables. This class of variables is particularly important because it forces analysts to think in dynamic rather than static terms. That is, one must inquire to what extent past events at time t-1 affect behavior now, time t, or are likely to affect future behavior at time t+1. There has been little research over time in the comparative study of foreign policy and this category explicitly requires it. However, we would stress that all of the variable categories in our framework can and should be thought of in this fashion.

Other's policies is the variable category that includes the actions of other international actors directed at the society or societies under analysis. Manifestations of this category surveyed in Chapter XII are hostile acts, threats, foreign support, and visits of heads of state.

This class of variables, along with the previous class of linkage variables and the next category, systemic variables, provide a conceptual connection between the comparative study of foreign policy and the analysis of international systems. To the extent that a group of states' foreign policies can be explained by looking just at linkages, other's policies, and systemic factors without considering the internal attributes of the states, the analysis is one of international interactions at the level of the system comprised by the states under analysis. Each state under study is treated as a whole or "billiard ball," whose movement is determined by the activity of the other balls, for one does not inquire into internal characteristics. It is important to link the study of international systems and subsystems to the comparative study of foreign policy. The three classes of variables (linkages, policies of others, and systemic variables) do this in a straightforward fashion. A study which begins at the system level of analysis but, in an effort to offer a complete explanation of the behavior in question, also considers the influence of variables ranging from the individual to the cultural categories, immediately becomes a study of comparative foreign policy.

Systemic variables comprise the final category of direct causal factors considered in the framework. They represent the sociopolitical and physical environment of the actor, such as its geographical position, number of neighbors, and characteristics of the international system at a given point in time, like its degree of conflict, organization in alliances, or number of members. At any given point in time the systemic variables are constant for a given country, but over time these factors can and do change. As Chapter XIII demonstrates, there has been a considerable amount of research into the influence of the systemic context on the foreign policy behavior of states.

These variable categories are conceptually different, not only because they name various factors that may determine the foreign policy of any actor, but because these factors are themselves different in two important ways. First, as Figure 6

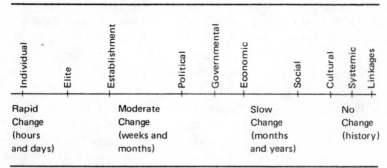

Figure 6: MAXIMUM RATES OF CHANGE IN VARIABLE CATEGORIES

suggests, each type of variable has a different possible rate of change. A given leader can be changed as rapidly as the time it takes to pull a trigger, whereas the cultural patterns of nations change very slowly over years and decades. Linkages are not open to change at all since they represent past behavior which, once done, cannot be removed from the public record. Second, as Figure 7 suggests, each type of variable is more or less removed from the actual act of deciding upon a foreign policy undertaking. Most directly related to this choice are variables tied to the decision-making process and the individual participants themselves. Farthest removed are cultural patterns of the society at large and the environmental variables. These two basic differences in the types of factors that cause foreign policy suggest that explanations of specific decisions or short-term policy behavior changes will probably use "close-in" variables that can change rapidly, like the categories of individual and elite variables. Studies of broad, long-term policy trends will most likely be explained in terms of slower changing, distant variables like the governmental, economic, and even past behavior or the previous linkages of the actor.

Two more aspects of the framework must be mentioned. The first is the influence of the *decision-making process* itself. As the framework suggests, we also consider this to be a variable category that intervenes between the eleven independent variable classes and the dependent variable of foreign policy. Past theoretical work has focused on decision-making variables to a great extent.[6] In Chapter XIV we examine the impact of such decision-making variables as crisis situations, the nature of the issue, and the decision-maker's images of foreign policy. It is important that the comparative study of foreign policy try to integrate the decision-making approach with other types of research, and we believe that putting decision-making and individual variables in our framework alerts the researcher to this task.

The final aspect of the framework is the two *feedback loops* leading from foreign policy to the actor and to the

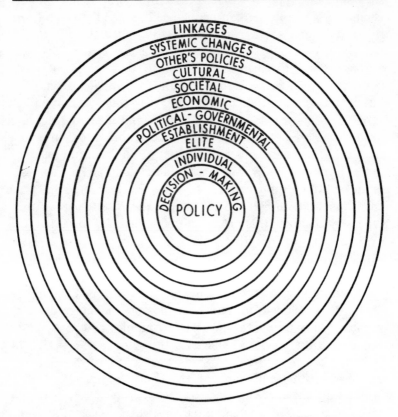

Figure 7: **SOCIAL DISTANCE OF CAUSAL VARIABLES FROM ACTUAL POLICY CHOICE**

international environment of the actor. The study of foreign policy has tended to neglect asking the vital question: What difference does foreign policy make for the acting state and the international system? These feedback loops emphasize the importance of this issue. When we do research on feedback, we treat foreign policy patterns as the independent variable and we ask what effect they have on the actor's structures and processes and the events within its environment, which are now treated as dependent variables. In Chapter XV we find that foreign policy has an impact on domestic politics, public opinion, and the international system in terms of its level of tension and the performance of international organizations.

Thus, we regard our framework as an heuristic device which is useful for integrating and comparing from one point of view a wide variety of research on foreign policy. It permits us to get away from an ad hoc listing of findings and propositions. It should be clear after our discussion of the framework that it is not a theory in the sense of that term as developed in Chapter I. Our framework has no deductive organization, nor does it present testable hypotheses. It is nothing more than an organizing device and as such it reflects the state of the field which, we have pointed out, is very poorly developed in terms of middle-range and general theory.

On the other hand, our framework is not devoid of theoretical uses. It can be very quickly adapted for integrating factor theories of foreign policy behavior. Thus, Figure 2 of the first chapter—where foreign policy consistency is hypothesized to be caused by leadership experience, cultural pluralism and external threats—relates the dependent variable (consistency) to variables from the individual, societal, and other's policies categories. In fact, it is this link between our framework and the state of "theory" in foreign policy studies, which is largely of the factor type, that has permitted us to write this *Survey*.

In our view, the prospects of theory-building in the comparative study of foreign policy are quite good. With respect to the feedback loops—the impact of the actor's behavior on itself and its environment—some form of cybernetic or adaptation theory is likely.[7] The basic theoretical questions would seek to know how variations in foreign policy behavior are related to variations in the performance of basic structures of the actor (e.g., its economy and political system) or to variations in the features of international systesm (e.g., extent of alliance aggregation). In dealing with the formulation of foreign policy as influenced by the eleven independent variables and the intervening variable class of the decision-making process we think that some form of exchange theory developed out of microeconomics or social psychology will be found most useful.[8] In this instance, the basic theoretical questions will center on how individual and group actors interact in more or less rewarding transactions to influence each other's behavior in the foreign policy-making process.

As we have had occasion to mention throughout this chapter, the propositions reported in this *Survey* are organized in terms of the framework. Thus, Chapters III through XIII will focus on each of the independent variables in turn, relating each of them to foreign policy outputs. The fourteenth chapter is devoted to the intervening variables of the decision-making process, and the fifteenth Chapter includes propositions about the two feedback loops.

In addition, there is an internal organization to each chapter. As far as has been possible, the propositions in each chapter are in the same order according to the kind of foreign policy output: the first proposition in each chapter usually deals with foreign policy formulation; the second, with foreign conflict behavior; the third, with United Nations voting; and so on. This scheme makes it easier for the reader to follow a particular type of behavior through the eleven independent variables, noting the effect of each on that output. The subject index at the end of the volume will also help in this respect.

NOTES

1. *Public Affairs Information Service, Social Science and Humanities Index, International Political Science Abstracts, ABS Guide to Recent Publications in the Social and Behavioral Sciences,* and *ABC Political Science.*

2. Studies listed in the bibliography and, thus, works surveyed in this volume, are referred to in this fashion to reduce footnotes. References to other works that are not empirical comparative foreign policy studies are cited in these traditional footnotes at the end of each chapter.

3. E. E. Azar, "Analysis of International Events," *Peace Research Reviews* IV (November 1970).

4. R. Burrowes, "Multiple Time-Series Analysis of Nation-Level Data," *Comparative Political Studies* II (January 1970): 465-480.

5. Lester W. Milbrath, *Political Participation* (Chicago: Rand McNally, 1965).

6. Richard C. Snyder et al. (eds.) *Foreign Policy Decision-Making* (New York: Free Press, 1962); and Joseph Frankel, *The Making of Foreign Policy: An Analysis of Decision-Making* (New York: Oxford University Press, 1963).

7. Karl W. Deutsch, *The Nerves of Government* (New York: Free Press, 1963); and James N. Rosenau, *The Adaptation of National Societies* (New York: McCaleb-Seiler, 1970).

8. See, for example, Robert Curry and L. I. Wade, *A Theory of Political Exchange* (Englewood Cliffs, N.J.: Prentice-Hall, 1969); and Sidney R. Waldman, *Foundations of Political Action: An Exchange Theory of Politics* (Boston: Little, Brown, 1972).

Chapter III

\
INDIVIDUAL VARIABLES

We begin our *Survey* at the most concrete level of analysis, the level closest to the actual foreign policy decision. This section recognizes one of the basic tenets of behavioralism: that the individual, far from being a mechanism manipulated by forces such as the "national interest" or "power relationships," is a significant independent factor in the decision-making process. His perceptual screen, his emotions, his personality, and his social background are all independent variables that may affect a nation's foreign policy behavior.

PROPOSITION 1:   *The images of decision-makers correspond to the foreign policy outputs of their nations.*
    Drawing on the theoretical work of Kenneth Boulding, several scholars have studied the extent to which the images of officials are translated into the foreign policy acts of their states. In a comparative case study of Sweden and Norway between 1940 and 1949, Burgess (1968: 160) concludes that

"images and outcomes corresponded very closely, and potential mediating factors were not sufficiently powerful to alter the outcome." This conclusion is based on Burgess' finding that the difference in the images of alliances between the two countries led directly to the failure of negotiations between them to establish a Scandanavian Defense Commission and to the decision of Norway to join NATO.

Choucri (1969a: 15) confirms the proposition for the nonaligned nations. In a content analysis of the speeches of Nehru, Nasser, and Sukarno at the conferences of Bogor, Bandung and Belgrade, she finds a congruent relationship between the images of the environment of these leaders and the acts of their respective nations. It is interesting that her research shows more congruence between images and concrete acts than between images and officially stated policies, suggesting that the latter are not a good indication of the intentions of policy-makers.

Affective attitudes towards other actors in the environment are not the same thing as images. Choucri (1969a: 15) finds no congruency between leaders' attitudes and foreign policy output. She is supported by a diachronic analysis of Indonesia between 1962 and 1970. The shift in Indonesia's general foreign policy stance from emphasis on independence to emphasis on development cannot be explained in terms of a change in attitudes that saw hostility in the outside world, because these remained substantially the same during the period of the shift in policy (Weinstein, 1972: 376-377).

PROPOSITION 2: *There is a positive relationship between perceptions of threat and hostility and expression of hostility.*

Drawing on psychology's stimulus-response theory, scholars have studied crisis situations. They have found that in the six weeks prior to World War I, if the decision-makers of one of the involved nations (Britain, France, Germany, Russia, Serbia, Austria-Hungary) perceived hostility and felt threatened, they reciprocated the hostility (Zinnes, 1966:

487; 1968: 110; North, Brody, and Holsti, 1964: 6, 9). Implicit in this finding are several others. One is that if hostility is expressed by one nation, decision-makers of the target nation will perceive it and will feel threatened (Zinnes, 1966: 487). A second is that when a leader perceives hostility, he is "capable of identifying the offending state and then expressing hostility toward it, rather than displacing *vis-á-vis* some third state" (Zinnes, 1968: =110). A third implication is the inherent possibility of a spiral of hostile actions as the reciprocity turns into a vicious cycle. This possibility is confirmed by North, Brody, and Holsti (1964: 10), who find that the frequency of perceptions and expressions of hostility rose uniformly through time for the members of the Dual Alliance and the Triple Entente. This is also confirmed by Hilton (1971: 256-257), who finds in the data a Markov chain process, in which the value of a variable depends on its own value at a previous point in time. His finding is that the expression of hostility by decision-makers in the prewar crisis is a function of their expressions of hostility in the two days prior (p <.001 for both alliances). That is, if a decision-maker makes threats one day, he must make even greater threats the next time in order to have any effect; this is clearly an escalatory process.

In this proposition we have an instance of a different treatment of the data leading to different conclusions, a possibility discussed in Chapter I. Hilton (1971: 260) omitted Serbia from his research and transformed the data for reasons that need not concern us here. He found that the perception of hostility is not related to the expression of hostility at the same time. However, for the Triple Entente nations, there is a significant relationship at a time lag of two and three days, but no corresponding relationship for the Dual Alliance.

Evidently, foreign policy-makers are able to separate their own egos from the state; that is, acts directed toward the nation as a whole are not seen as acts directed at them personally. Although, as we have seen, perceptions of hostility toward the state are related to expressions of hostility, it is not true that the decision-maker's perceptions of himself as the object of hostility are related to expressions of hostility (Zinnes, 1962: 240-241). However, perceptions of himself as the object of hostility are positively related to the frequency of the decision-maker's statements of goals and policy, though the finding is not statistically significant.

Research on this proposition has been brought up to date in one of the few empirical studies that have been published on the Vietnam war. Analyzing statements of top decision-makers from July 1964 to December 1967, the period of major escalation, Mitchell (1971: 55-56) finds that during periods of stress, when perceptions of hostility are high, United States statements on negotiations, on the level of U.S. military activity, and on the possibility of reciprocal de-escalation are much less conciliatory (i.e., more hostile) than during periods of nonstress.

PROPOSITION 3:   *There is a positive relationship between decision-makers' perceptions of hostility and the level of violence of their nation's foreign policy acts.*

When hostility is perceived, a verbal expression of hostility is not the only reaction provoked. In addition, concrete hostile acts are taken. As the perceptions of hostility in the pre-World War I crisis increased, the level of violence of a nation's actions increased (North, 1967: 122). One of the manifestations of this violence was the mobilization of troops, which North, Brody, and Holsti (1964: 13) find increasing with increased perceived hostility. However, these findings are modified somewhat by another study by the same scholars. Analyzing the proposition separately for the members of the Triple Entente and the members of the Dual Alliance, Holsti, North, and Brody (1968: 157) find that the association between perceptions of hostility and hostile actions was high for the members of the Triple Entente, which became involved only late in the crisis, and much lower for the members of the Dual Alliance, which were engaged for the entire crisis period. This modification shows the danger of aggregating all nations in a study without looking at subsets of the population under analysis. Another explanation for the difference in findings is that the dependent variable, hostile actions, is operationalized in different ways in the two studies, reflecting the field's lack of consensus on definitions, as discussed in Chapter I.

In the Cold War, perceived threat has been strongly related to hostile foreign policy acts. One begins to realize the importance of this variable, perceptions of the individual, when it becomes a major determinant of whether or not a government leader will press the nuclear button. Schwartz (1967: 479) reports that the crisis-initiation actions of Soviet policy-makers in eight crises between 1950 and 1964 are positively associated with increased felt threat to those individuals. Sigal (1970: 149-154) finds that the hostile actions of the People's Republic of China during the three Formosa Straits crises (1954-1955, 1958, 1962) can be accounted for in terms of the threats which her leaders perceived and their efforts to undermine or eliminate them.

Apparently Proposition 3 is applicable to noncrisis as well as crisis situations. Analyzing 32 foreign policy decisions of a number of states in the twentieth century (n is not specified), Michael Haas (1969a: 85-86) observes that the number of violent foreign policy options considered prior to a decision as well as the number of decisions involving violence is high when the decision-makers have previous hostile views of the target nation. This study tells us something not only about foreign policy acts, but also about the process of formulating foreign policy.

A major implication of Proposition 3 is that the stimulus-response mode of action of decision-makers escalates the level of hostility; that is, the hostile acts taken do not remain at the same level of hostility throughout a crisis situation. In a longitudinal study of the Middle East between 1953 and 1965, Lambelet (1971: 166) confirms this expectation, finding a positive relationship between the amount of threat perceived and the level of reaction in terms of escalating the arms race. Israel has felt most threatened and has escalated the most, in terms of increases in defense expenditures; Iraq has felt least threatened and Egypt and Syria occupy intermediate positions. While defense expenditures may increase as a response to crisis, the actual level of military activity during that crisis may be reduced. This was the case in the Vietnam war during periods of stress from 1964 through 1967 (Mitchell, 1971: 57). Obviously this escalation hypothesis needs more testing.

PROPOSITION 4:   *As stress increases in a crisis situation, the decision-maker's perceptions of the factors involved in the decision-making process change also.*

The model of rational decision-making posits that a government official defines the situation at hand, selects his goals, and then searches for and chooses the "best" alternative to achieve those goals. Stress on the individual can affect this process. In his study of the pre-World War I crisis, Holsti (1965: 98) makes this statement:

In a crisis situation, decision-makers will tend to perceive their own range of alternatives [and that of their allies] to be more restricted than those of their adversaries; that is, they will perceive their own decision-making to be characterized by *necessity and closed* options, whereas those of the adversary are characterized by *open* choices.

In the six weeks prior to the first World War and in three of eight crises between the Soviet Union and the United States between 1950 and 1964, as the stress built upon decision-makers, they perceived an expanding range of alternatives open to adversaries or potential adversaries (Holsti, 1965: 105). This finding was confirmed for the Dual Alliance, but not for the Triple Entente.

Stress also affects the perceptions of which factors are important in a crisis situation. Time became a more salient factor as stress increased on the decision-makers of the five European powers before World War I (Holsti, 1965: 95). The immediate, rather than the distant, future became the pressing concern (Holsti, 1965: 97). And the capability of a nation relative to its adversaries became a less important factor in the decision to go to war as stress increased; more important was the injury that had been done to the decision-maker's state (Zinnes, North, and Koch, 1961: 470; Holsti and North, 1965: 169).

Stress also affects the decision-maker's perception of the situation in terms of the amount of hostility perceived in the environment. Zinnes (1962: 241; 1966: 487) reports that as the perception of threat of World War I leaders increased, they perceived that the number of hostile states and the amount of hostility in the environment were increasing also. In fact, the "index of injury" for all five nations at the time was highest at the two crisis stages—the local war between Austria and Serbia, and the start of the general war involving all five states (Holsti and North, 1965: 167).

Finally, stress may cause an actor to misperceive the actions of another, thus giving him an inaccurate definition of the situation. In the Formosa Straits crises, "even the suggestions of a powerful adversary come to resemble threats when their recipient takes into account capabilities as well as intentions in deciding what to do" (Sigal, 1970: 149).

In war, one of the factors that may *not* be misperceived during periods of stress is the level of the enemy's military activity. Perhaps this is because the normal intelligence operations continue to operate even during these crisis periods. This is the finding of Mitchell (1971: 53) in an analysis of United States perceptions of North Vietnamese and Viet Cong military actions. In fact, Mitchell (1971: 59) finds that perceptions more accurately reflect actual battle-field conditions during periods of stress.

In his study of eight Soviet-American crises between 1950 and 1964, Schwartz turns Proposition 4 around and uses perceptions of the situation as the independent variable. He states (1967: 482-483) that, as the Soviet officials perceive the military crisis resource balance to increasingly favor the

United States, they will feel increased threat (i.e., stress increases). And as American strategic and/or tactical preparedness is perceived to increase, the Soviets will perceive increases in the resolve of United States decision-makers (again, stress increases).

PROPOSITION 5:   *As stress increases in a crisis situation, there will be changes in the procedure of the decision-making process.*

Holsti's study of the 1914 crisis pays particular attention to the communication processes of crisis decision-making. He reports (1965: 114) that "the higher the stress in a crisis situation, the higher the proportion of intra-coalition—as against inter-coalition—communication." The messages sent among nations also become more stereotyped in their information content as stress increases (Holsti, 1965: 112). The channels through which these messages are sent become overloaded, and there is an increasing tendency to rely upon extraordinary or improvised channels of communication (Holsti, 1965: 107, 113). Also, the reaction time to communications from the adversary (i.e., the rate of response to stimulus) becomes shorter as a crisis becomes more intense (Hilton, 1971: 257).

Crises seem to have an effect on the formulation of foreign policy statements. In his study of the Vietnam war, Mitchell (1971: 54, 57) finds that "U.S. statements tend to be expressed in more certain terms with less possibility of change" during periods of stress. Also, civilian policy-making and military policy-making are more tightly meshed during crises, if statements can be taken as an indication: Mitchell reports that statements of the two groups on the level of American military activity are indistinguishable when decision-makers are under stress, even though there are great differences during noncrisis periods.

One aspect of the decision-making process that does not seem to change in crisis is the degree of centralization. Schwartz's study (1967) finds that increasing perceived threat is not related to an increase in the centralization of the decision-making process. One might speculate that the explanation lies in the fact that foreign policy-making is centralized at all times, certainly much more so than domestic policy-making.

Miscellaneous Findings

Miscellaneous findings will be listed at the end of most of the chapters of the *Survey*. These are single findings that could not be integrated into the generalized propositions. They are, of course, of the same scientific validity as all the findings reported.

In a study of France, Germany, Japan, and the United States from the late nineteenth to the middle of the twentieth century, Benjamin and Edinger (1971: 14) find that "normative role perceptions" is one of six variable groups that show a small to moderate relationship (Cramer's V from .00 to .44) with military control of foreign policy.

Analyzing recipient attitudes toward foreign aid, Andreas (1969: 176) makes the statement:

"when power of recipient nation is perceived to be high, one will exert most effort to decrease one's 'costs' in a reciprocal or exchange relationship; when power is perceived to be low, one will exert most effort to increase 'rewards'."

Russett (1968b: 97-98) finds a relationship between the economic and personal ties to another country of legislators in Great Britain and the United States and their responsiveness to the needs of that country.

The relationship of perceived hostility to the interactions between nations before World War I has not yet been established. Zinnes (1966: 491) finds that there is not a *negative* relationship between the two variables, but she does not test the hypothesis to see whether the relationship is positive or whether there is simply no relationship.

How does the influence of individual variables on the formulation of foreign policy compare to the influence of other factors? There is only one study that makes this kind of comparison. Rosenau (1968: 45) finds that individual variables are less of a factor than role variables in the foreign policy preferences of U.S. Senators during the Acheson and Dulles periods.

Evaluation

The studies surveyed in this section validate the notion that the individual plays a vital role in the foreign policy-making process, and that he is not a passive instrument through which the play of "power" or "national interest" is acted out. More specifically, they show that the decision-maker reacts in various ways to the hostility directed at him: he becomes more hostile himself, the acts he chooses are more violent, and his perceptions of the environment change. The policy implications of these propositions are obvious: in a crisis situation there is danger of an escalating spiral of hostility as decision-makers on each side perceive and react to the acts of their opponent.

The greatest strength of these propositions is that the research on them has been methodologically rigorous and replicated. Eleven separate works of the "Stanford group" are included in this section, all using data from content analysis of documents of key World War I leaders. The most glaring weakness of the propositions is that their support derives mainly from studies of only one crisis situation; the other studies in the section are rather isolated and they have not been replicated. Thus our ability to generalize beyond the prewar crisis must remain limited until the research on other crises is replicated and made more comparable. Also, the propositions should be studied in non-crisis situations to show exactly what differences if any exist between crisis and noncrisis decision-making.

The specific independent variables used in the research surveyed are individual perceptions and stress on the individual. Other variables such as the attitudes, the personality, and the social background of the decision-maker are also useful explanatory factors but few scholars have studied comparatively their effect on foreign policy output. Future research must look at these variables in both crises and noncrisis situation.[1]

NOTES

1. For an insightful, but nonsystematic, survey of psychological variables, see Joseph De Rivera, *The Psychological Dimension of Foreign Policy* (Columbus, Ohio: Charles E. Merrill, 1968).

Chapter IV

ELITE VARIABLES

The individuals who influence foreign policy come and go, but their aggregate characteristics may remain quite stable over a long period of time. Some observers note that the State Department has tended to recruit the same type of people for many years. Others try to identify certain aggregate characteristics that enable one to distinguish a particular foreign policy elite from previous or succeeding elites. This section is devoted to propositions that analyze the influence of the distribution among the elite of social background, economic status, party membership, and the like on a nation's foreign policy output.

PROPOSITION 6:   *The basis of recruitment of foreign policy elites is related to the process of formulation of foreign policy.*
Each nation of the world recruits its foreign policy elite on the basis of certain criteria; these are rarely stated as official

policy, but are always implicit in the process of selecting individuals to be the official representatives of the government. One can look at the effect of recruitment criteria at the various stages of foreign policy formulation, the criteria being defined in terms of Parsons' pattern variables. Analyzing recruitment in 45 nations in the 1960s, McGowan (1970: 219) finds that "the more important achievement critieria are in foreign policy elite recruitment, the more pluralistic will be the policy articulation process and the more conflictful will be the policy formation process."

Bonham (1970: 335-336) has carried out much more limited research on the proposition. He looks at only one region and at the formation of attitudes towards one particular policy: for parliamentarians of Norway, Sweden, and Denmark in 1967, recruitment based on initial favorable attitudes and on age is a better explanation than participation in supranational organizations for the attitudes of those individuals toward supranational issues.

To say that there are certain basic criteria for recruitment is not to say that all members of the elite are the same. For example, given the fact that recruitment is based on achievement criteria, there will still be differences in terms of religion, age, ethnicity, and other social background characteristics. These differences will be reflected in foreign policy acts of the elite. Over five different sessions in the U.S. Congress, for example, Catholics tend to be more internationalist than Protestants in voting on foreign aid (Rieselbach, 1964: 579-587). Internationalism is associated with representatives from eastern and Pacific states, from urban areas, and from districts of high educational level and socioeconomic status. There has been a switch in the effect of ethnicity: before World War II, representatives from high ethnic (percentage of German and Italian ancestry) districts were less internationalist in their voting, but since the war the reverse has been true.

PROPOSITION 7:   *The roles occupied by members of the elite are related to their foreign policy actions and attitudes.*

A major argument of this book is that single-variable explanations are inadequate to explain something as complex as foreign policy. That the basis on which a person is recruited affects his foreign policy acts does not mean that he is preprogrammed when he takes office; role variables also have an effect on his actions and attitudes.

Rosenau (1968: 45) makes this clear in his study of the U.S. Senate in two time periods; 1949-1952 and 1953-1956. His conclusion is that role variables are more important than individual variables in guiding the behavior of senators; members of the Foreign Relations Committee had different attitudes toward the actions of the Secretary of State than other senators. In his study of the House of Representatives, Rieselbach (1964: 580-581) discovers the same pattern with respect to a different foreign policy attitude: members of the House Committee on Foreign Affairs have been more internationalist in their voting on foreign aid than other representatives.

The role variable of party membership is related to these same two attitudes. Rosenau (1968: 45) finds that a senator's party membership determined his behavior toward the Secretary of State; and Rieselbach (1964: 579), examining a twenty-year period which encompasses World War II, finds that party affiliation was associated with voting on foreign aid in the House of Representatives at the beginning of this period, but that by the end of this period, there was no statistical difference between Republicans and Democrats on foreign aid voting.

Holsti presents a finding which modifies the Rosenau and Rieselbach studies. We say "modifies" and not "disconfirms" because his dependent variable is different and the individuals studied were the very top leaders and not legislators. Holsti (1970: 309) reports that in 1914, for the policy-makers of France, Britain, Germany, Russia, Austria-Hungary, and

Serbia, the foreign policy office occupied does not account for any variation among individual perceptions of hostility.

Evaluation

Not much of an evaluation can be made when there are only five comparative studies relevant to this variable cluster. Considering the extent to which the concept of "elite" is employed in political science and sociology, the small amount of research on this variable is surprising. But the Rosenau article is an excellent start in that it tries to determine the influence of elite role variables relative to individual variables among the senatorial elite in the United States. Both it and the Rieselbach study must be extended to foreign policy elites of other nations.

Social background data on foreign policy elites are easy to collect from many published sources. Attitudes and beliefs of elites, and in particular the degree of consensus that the elite manifests, can be inferred from the content analysis of elite statements. Elite deicsion-making behavior can be examined via the comparative case study approach. Many of the research questions and methodologies developed in community power studies at the local level seem very suited to the study of foreign policy elites.[1] Much more work needs to be done in this area for, as our survey shows, we know very little of a comparative nature about the elites around the world who make foreign policy and their impact upon the actual policies chosen.

NOTES

1. See in this regard Nelson W. Polsby, *Community Power and Political Theory* (New Haven: Yale University Press, 1963); and Terry N. Clark (ed.) *Community Structure and Decision-Making: Comparative Analysis* (San Francisco: Chandler, 1968).

Chapter V

ESTABLISHMENT VARIABLES

Two nations may have entirely opposite types of government and yet be quite similar in the way they organize their foreign policy-making processes. The result might be foreign policies that are more like each other than would be otherwise expected. In other words, variables such as the number of organizations typically involved in a decision, their degree of bureaucratization, their relative power on different issues, and their procedures for policy-making have an important impact on foreign policy behavior. These types of variables have been grouped under the heading "establishment" in this section.

PROPOSITION 8: *Conflict among various policy-making groups determines the level at which decisions are made.*

An important question from the standpoint of normative democratic theory is what are the conditions that favor military control of foreign policy. Benjamin and Edinger

(1971:19) try to answer this question by analyzing 62 cases of military participation in foreign policy decisions in France, Germany, Japan, and the United States from the late nineteenth century to the middle of the twentieth. One of their findings is that when there is intense conflict between military and civilian groups on issues, the outcome with respect to who has greater influence on the adopted policy favors the military.

Another aspect of this proposition is the effect of bureaucratic conflict on the level within the civilian hierarchy at which decisions are made. Hilsman (1967: 543, 546) has reported on this phenomenon in seven cases of decision-making during the Kennedy administration. He finds that a "consequence of the multiplicity of constituencies involved in policy-making is that more and more problems are thrown into the White House." In addition, "what might be called the 'jurisdictional' effect of bureaucracy tends to increase still more the number of problems that must elbow their way right to the very top." A modifying factor, however, is time: Hilsman finds that the longer a policy debate continues, the more organizations and groups will become involved until the issue becomes a public debate and the decision-making power of the top leaders becomes curtailed.

PROPOSITION 9:   *The greater the degree of centralization in a government, the more likely that the nation will be involved in foreign conflict.*

Gregg and Banks (1965: 614) report that "the presence of strong executive *leadership* is frequently accompanied by both diplomatic and violent foreign conflict." Their study covers 115 countries listed in *A Cross-Polity Survey* and uses five foreign conflict variables. If centralization can be equated with strong executive leadership, then Quincy Wright (1964: 159) supports their statement. He finds that the highly centralized government is more likely to be involved in war than the decentralized government. Wright (1964: 160) also notes that nations in the process of centralizing or decentralizing will also have a tendency to be involved in war.

PROPOSITION 10:   *The greater the policy conflict among decision-making groups, the smaller are the chances that the policy will be successful.*

It is one thing for a government to adopt a policy and quite another to put it into effect. Conflict in the process of formulating policy makes chances for successful implementation more problematic. One reason for this is that conflict implies that there will be compromise, thus watering down the policy. Another is that the high degree of publicity that a policy receives when it is the object of conflict exposes the underlying, as opposed to the stated, objectives of the policy, with particularly adverse effects in foreign policy.

In a comparative case study, Brzezinski and Huntington (1963: 386-387) conclude that, because compromise was not necessary in the Soviet Union, Soviet foreign policy toward Hungary in 1956 was more likely to succeed; the necessity for compromise in the United States was a factor in the failure of American policy in Cuba at the time of the Bay of Pigs invasion. In an effort to improve their bargaining positions, decision-making groups in the United States "leaked" ambiguous assessments of the situation in the three Formosa Straits crises; these leaks were perceived as threats by Peking, though they were not intended as such, and they thus raised the level of hostility and contributed to the failure of U.S. policy.

The United States has been less successful in minimizing the number and visibility of the "strings" attached to its foreign aid than has the Soviet Union, because the former is subject to the legislature's control of appropriations while the latter is faced with no such pressure (Walters, 1970: 168). Also

"the visibility and frankness of such debate in the United States makes it much more difficult for America to present the image of a positive, selfless aid program to the third world than it is for the Soviet Union where domestic opposition to aid and debates on aid issues are muted" [Walters, 1970: 235].

The effect of both of these factors, Walters concludes, has been to reduce the effectiveness of the U.S. aid program in comparison with the Soviet program.

PROPOSITION 11: *The greater the expertise and ability of bureaucratic groups, the greater are the chances that foreign policy will be successful.*

There are two aspects to this proposition. The first is that the nature of the bureaucracy of the actor affects the success of that nation's acts. The second is that the nature of the bureaucracy of a target nation affects the success of acts directed by another state at that nation. We will deal with each separately.

The character of leadership, in terms of the amount of attention given to a policy by top leaders and the degree of experience of individuals, was a factor in the success of Soviet policy in Hungary and in the failure of American policy in Cuba (Brzezinski and Huntington, 1964: 384-387). This factor is also important in the success of diplomatic protests. When leaders are inexperienced and/or give certain policies little of their attention, afterthought rather than forethought characterizes the policy formulation process. The result is error in estimating the costs of the protest and a diminished value for the protest. This has been found to be the case in five American diplomatic protests made between 1900 and 1935 (McKenna, 1962: 195, 197).

This research of McKenna's brings up the question of the effect of diplomatic expertise on the success of foreign policy. In a comparative case study, Craig (1961: 107-108) finds that the failure of the Italian Fascist and German Nazi governments to understand or take advantage of the uses of negotiation was a cause of their foreign policy failures, whereas the Soviet government's ability to devise new techniques of negotiation and adapt old ones to their purposes helped to consolidate their foreign policy successes. In a comparative case study focusing just on the United States in Laos, Cuba, and Vietnam, George et al. (1971:

231-232) report that the success of U.S. coercive diplomacy depends in part on the leaders' skill in devising specific tactics; the content and timing of ultimatums, the balance between coercion and conflict management, the timing and content of threats, the timing of negotiations, and the timing and content of the carrot and the stick.

Turning now to the second subset of Proposition 11, we find two confirming studies. Ness (1969: 60-62), examining five cases of land reform imposed by the United States, finds that one of the conditions under which the foreign policy of a superordinate nation can have a decisive effect on social change in a subordinate nation is the existence of effective local organization for implementing the reforms. And Walters (1970: 234), in his comparison of Soviet and American economic aid programs, reports that the problems encountered in these activities are a factor of "the difficulties experienced by LDC's in financing local costs, providing services, and mobilizing adequate supplies of materials and labor."

Miscellaneous Findings

In his study of foreign policy-making in 45 nations, McGowan (1970: 216) finds that "the greater the degree of institutionalization of foreign policy establishments, the greater will be the influence of achievement criteria in the recruitment of foreign policy elites."

In a cross-sectional analysis of 99 and 103 United Nations members in the 1960s, Vincent (1971: 489) finds that the factor of "executive leadership" accounts for six percent of the variance in both the "southern voting" and "U.N. intervention" dimensions of U.N. voting.

Evaluation

Most of the findings reported in this chapter depend upon comparative case studies of the United States and the Soviet Union for their validity. Although these are good analyses, our confidence in their findings is limited until comparative studies on a larger number of nations using more rigorous controls are conducted.

We would like to see research on establishment variables that is issue-specific. Are these types of factors more influential in noncrisis situations than in crises, or on some issues but not on others? Does the ability of a bureaucracy to affect foreign policy depend on the issue? Does the nature and the extent of organizational conflict vary with the issue, and does this affect the policy outcome?

From our point of view it is entirely appropriate to consider foreign policy an aspect of the broader problem of public policy formation. While the "goods" created by a successful foreign policy (such as "security" or "peace") are in many respects less tangible than the "goods" delivered by domestic health, education, and housing programs; in other cases, such as trade negotiations or foreign aid agreements, they provide concrete public rewards to the concerned sectors of society. Schools of public administration in both their teaching and research have tended to neglect the organizational and administrative aspects of foreign and defense policy. Developments in organization theory, systems analysis, and the measurement and explanation of public policy outputs offer a rich store of insight and evidence for the student of foreign policy. Moreover, the traditional normative concerns of students of public administration in such issues as the possible conflict between democratic participation and the "administrative state" are worthy of the attention of students of comparative foreign policy.

The foreign policy establishment may also be vital to the explanation of foreign policy behavior. A good working hypothesis is that particular foreign policies are adopted because they benefit some group interest or sector of society. Foreign policies, as we have noted, deliver valued public goods. It may well be that research will discover that it is the organizations that make and implement foreign policy that are the main beneficiaries of a nation's policies. Clearly, more comparative research on foreign policy establishments is needed.

Chapter VI

POLITICAL VARIABLES

Traditional theory on foreign policy has postulated that a nation's international situation—its position within the international system—is the major determinant of its foreign policy behavior. Recently, however, scholars have emphasized that the domestic environment is at least as important a factor. This perspective is reflected in the framework used in this survey. A major part of that domestic environment, of course, is the set of phenomena that we label "political." This includes variables such as the activities of pressure groups, the amount of domestic political conflict, the competition among politicians, the nature of the party system, and the level of political development.

PROPOSITION 12:   *Variations in domestic political variables over time affect the formulation of a nation's foreign policy.*

The statement in the previous paragraph that domestic politics is considered a major factor in foreign policy-making represents more than our impression of the "state of the field" or an expression of the theoretical biases of scholars. It is an hypothesis that has been empirically tested. East and Gregg (1967: 265) find that the foreign policy acts of 82 nations are "systematically rather than randomly associated with their domestic conditions." They operationalize "acts" as conflictual and cooperative behavior and, although this is only part of foreign policy behavior, it is nonetheless a start in validating this important hypothesis. Jensen takes the proposition one step further in a more limited study. Examining the national security policy process in Germany, Japan, and Italy, Jensen (1969b: 322) finds that the internal environment is a *more* important factor that the external environment in the formulation of national security policy.

PROPOSITION 13:   *The degree of political competition affects the process of formulating foreign policy.*

Two studies examine the effect of political competition on the general process of policy formulation, and two others look at the effect of competition on the adoption of specific policies. In his research on 45 nations in the 1960s, McGowan (1970: 212, 242) finds a positive relationship between the degree of competitiveness of the party system and the influence of achievement criteria in the recruitment of foreign policy elites. Also, "the more competitive the party system, the more pluralistic will be the process of policy articulation and the more conflictful will be the process of policy formation." In turn, a greater degree of pluralism in policy articulation leads to more conflict in the persuasion stage of the process. In their comparative analysis of Germany, France, Japan, and the United States, Benajmin and Edinger (1971: 19) conclude that when mass political participation is restricted, there is a greater likelihood that the military will control the foreign policy process.

On a more specific level, when decision-makers have a high

probability of retaining office (i.e., when political competition is reduced), the number of violent options considered
prior to a decision is high. Intense desires for power and
achievement in these decision-makers make it more likely
that a violent option will be chosen. These are the findings of
a study of 32 foreign policy decisions of various nations by
Haas (1969a: 85-86). He is supported in this by Weinstein
(1972: 277-339), whose study of Indonesia reveals an
association between the degree of political competition and
the foreign policy stance adopted—in this case, either a policy
of independence or a policy of development.

PROPOSITION 14: *Public opinion is a limited but ever-present
constraint on policy-making whose impact varies
with the issue.*

A number of longitudinal case studies examine the
influence of public opinion on foreign policy formulation.
Clemens (1966: 63), in a longitudinal study of the period
1954-1964, finds that the demands of the Soviet public for
peace and prosperity were an influence, although never a
decisive one, on the formulation of arms control policy.
Bunker (1969: 296) reports that, despite the overwhelming
influence of the United States on Peru's foreign policy
(1958-1966), Peruvian interest groups could still influence
the policy-making process through political bargaining. Hilsman's work (1967: 547) on the Kennedy administration
indicates that the need to gain wide support for a policy
sometimes leads policy-makers to claim too much for it. This
need for support has varying effects on the process of policy
articulation: sometimes a clear and effective statement may
be required, and at other times ambiguity may be necessary.
This is not to say that the process of consensus-building
inhibits the foreign policy process, for Hilsman (1967: 549)
does find conditions where the need to build a consensus can
lead to effective assessment of policy alternatives: when the
subject is one on which the competing groups are knowledge-
able, when the interested constituencies within and outside

the government are well informed, and when relevant government officials are responsive to the decision and persuaded by it.

A major point of these findings of Hilsman is that the relationship of public opinion to foreign policy depends on the issue. Even within one issue-area, the effect of public opinion can vary under different conditions. McKenna (1962: 196), in his study of American diplomatic protests, finds no stable trend in U.S. history: domestic politics are at times a very important consideration when leaders formulate protests, and at other times they are irrelevant. Hoffman's findings (1967: 154) are the same: in 1935 public pressure had nothing to do with British economic sanctions against Italy, but in 1965 they were a major reason why sanctions were adopted against Rhodesia.

Two authors have found that certain policies do not succeed without public support. In their study of United States foreign policy in Laos, Cuba and Vietnam, George, et al. (1971: 216) observe that adequate domestic political support is one of the conditions favoring the success of U.S. coercive diplomacy. Schwartz (1967: 488), analyzing eight Soviet-American crises, concludes that "changes in crisis policy will be more easily accomplished if these changes can be rationalized within extant political-military doctrines."

Theorists have often separated "the people" from their governments, claiming that the former are more of an influence for peace than the latter. Though public opinion exercised a greater influence on policy in Great Britain, France, and the United States than in Germany and Eastern Europe before World War I, it cannot be said that in any of these countries the influence of public opinion is positively correlated with a more peaceful or more enlightened policy (Schmitt, 1961: 329). However, public opinion does have a relationship with war and peace. In research focusing on the period 1955 to 1960, Haas (1968b: 109) reports: "When attitudes are subject to much change over time, are poorly linked, or are transactionally out of phase with the external environment, international aggression seems nearly always to be imminent."

PROPOSITION 15: *There is little or no relationship between domestic conflict and foreign conflict at one point in time.*

One of the most extensively studied hypotheses in the comparative study of foreign policy is the relationship between domestic conflict and foreign conflict. This is the one area in which the construction of a body of cumulative research findings through replication is being achieved. This proposition and the next two deal with this topic. First we consider the general categories of conflict for all nations and at one point in time. Then we consider the effect of breaking down both conflict and nations into different types, but still at one point in time. Finally we examine the effect of a time lag on the hypothesis.

Seven studies find that there is little or no relationship between domestic instability and conflict and foreign conflict behavior at one point in time. Three of these studies are by Rummel. He finds no relationship between the two variables using 3,500 events taken from the *New York Times Index* and other sources for 77 nations for the period 1955-1957 (1963: 24); using 217 national attribute variables and 13 foreign conflict variables from the DON project for 77 nations in the period 1955-1957 (1968: 204-213); and using 236 foreign and domestic behavior variables from the DON data for 82 nations for 1955 (1967b: 197). Tanter (1966: 61) replicated Rummel's original analysis using an unspecified number of events from the *Times Index* and other sources for 83 nations for the period 1958-1960. He finds only a small relationship between domestic and foreign conflict, but he does report that the relationship increases with a time lag. East and Gregg (1967: 266) did a replication with the data from the DON project and also support the proposition for 82 nations (time period unspecified). Weeds (1970: 234) also uses the DON data, but for 59 nations and the years 1955-1960, and he comes to the same conclusion. Finally, Jensen (1969a: 205) taking his data on the two variables from the *Times Index* and *Deadline Data* for an unspecified number of cases of conflict between India and Pakistan (1947-1966), finds that there is only a weak relationship between domestic and foreign conflict.

Lest we feel too secure in our knowledge, we report the findings of two studies which modify or tend to disconfirm Proposition 15. The Feierabends, on the basis of a study of 84 nations for the years 1955-1961, conclude (1969: 150) that internal political unrest is the only variable that is "possibly" related to external aggression for all nations. They are less emphatic than Collins (1967: 116), whose study covers 33 independent African states for the period 1963-1965 and which finds "a high degree of overall concomitant variation between domestic disorder and foreign conflict behavior."

PROPOSITION 16: *For certain classes of nations, there is a positive relationship between certain types of domestic conflict and certain types of foreign conflict behavior at one point in time.*

Breaking up foreign conflict into types, Collins (1967: 116-117) finds that in Black Africa domestic disorder is most directly related to formal diplomatic hostility and nonviolent hostile actions and moderately related to interference and hostility. He does not find (1967: 117) a relationship between domestic disorder and official military activities or unofficial antiforeign activities. Haas (1965: 323) makes the breakdown the other way, examining the types of domestic conflict for about 70 nations, and reports that of the three types of domestic social conflict—legitimate, anomic, and illegitimate—anomic conflict shows the closest relationship to foreign conflict, while the other two types show a lower, but still positive, correlation.

Gregg and Banks (1965: 614) break down both variables for 115 polities and report that "the political dimension, *consensus,* which accounts for most of the domestic conflict, does not account for diplomatic conflict, but is moderately associated with violent foreign conflict." Wright (1964: 164) also breaks down the variables and finds that the threat of civil war has been associated with a nation's involvement in foreign war.

Ivo and Rosalind Feierabend do not categorize the conflict variables but examine the proposition for different types of states. They conclude (1969: 163) that the nonmodern country which is sufficiently frustrated to be politically unstable has the strongest probability of also being externally aggressive; and the modern, satisfied country will be internally stable and externally nonaggressive, except for the major powers (United States, Soviet Union, Britain, France, and China).

The final support for this proposition is given in two studies by Wilkenfeld, who uses factor analysis to categorize types of conflict and types of nations. The analyses are replications of Rummel's and Tanter's work, in that they use the DON data for 74 nations for the period 1955-1960. The differences from the earlier studies lie in the fact that Wilkenfeld's papers are diachronic and they categorize the variables and the nations. For "personalist" nations, all types of internal conflict are related to foreign conflict of the "diplomatic" type (1971: 197-198); however, there is no relationship between the domestic conflict factor "internal war" and the foreign conflict factor "war" (1969: 151). For "centrist" nations, "internal war" is related to "war," and "turmoil" correlates with the foreign conflict factors "war," "diplomatic," and "belligerency" (1969: 153). For polyarchic nations, "turmoil" is realted to all types of foreign conflict behavior (1971: 201); "internal war," on the other hand, is not related to foreign conflict except of the "diplomatic" type, where a low negative correlation is found (1969: 153).

PROPOSITION 17:   *For certain classes of nations, there is a positive relationship between some types of domestic conflict and some types of foreign conflict behavior at a lag of one and/or two years.*

In support of this proposition, we have only the works of Wilkenfeld mentioned in the previous paragraph, plus a more recent study by Zinnes and Wilkenfled. We should, however, recall that Tanter, although he does not categorize the variables or the nations, does introduce a time lag and finds that the small relationship between domestic and foreign conflict does increase with that lag (1966: 61).

Wilkenfeld reports that for personalist nations, there is a significant correlation between the domestic conflict factor "internal war" and the foreign conflict factors "belligerency," one and two years later, and "war," two years later (1969: 151). For centrist nations, "internal war" is significantly correlated with "war" one and two years later (1969: 153), and internal conflict of the "revolutionary" type is related to all types of foreign conflict one and two years later (1971: 199). Also for centrist nations, there are significant relationships between "turmoil" and the foreign conflict factors "diplomatic" and "belligerency" one and two years later, and between "turmoil" and "war" two years later. For polyarchic nations, Wilkenfeld finds a disconfirming instance: there is no correlation between the domestic factors "revolutionary" and "subversive" and any of the types of foreign conflict at any time lag (1971: 200-201).

Zinnes and Wilkenfeld (1971: 186, 191, 206-207) carry the analysis of domestic and foreign conflict one step further by using as the dependent variable the *transition* from one level of foreign conflict to another. This article uses the same data as the two Wilkenfeld studies: 74 nations for 1955-1960. For all states, "the level of domestic conflict does not significantly affect a state's transition probability from one level of foreign conflict to another." There is one exception for all states: the domestic conflict factors of "internal war" and "turmoil" affect the escalation or de-escalation of the "belligerency" factor of foreign conflict. Also for all states, "when the level of domestic conflict coincides with the level of previous foreign conflict behavior, the tendency is to remain at the same level of foreing conflict behavior." Finally, there are some relationships for certain types of nations: for polyarchic states, internal warfare is related to the transition probabilities for belligerency, and for centrist states, domestic turmoil is related to the transition probabilities for belligerency.

PROPOSITION 18:   *The less the political unity of a state, the less are its aggressive tendencies.*

It is difficult for a government which does not have effective control over its citizens to wage war against others. Thus the infrequency of border wars and border claims in Africa is attributed, in a comparative study of several border disputes, to the fact that "effective government control has not yet become coterminous with the limits of the state" (Zartman, 1965: 161).

The size of the military establishment is one measure of a nation's aggressive tendencies; according to our proposition, we expect a negative relationship between political instability and size of the military. Only Terrell (1971: 343) has studied this relationship in a time-lag analysis of 75 nations (with a population greater than 800,000 and soveriegn in 1955) covering the post-World War II period. The expectation is not supported; very little of the variance in military expenditures as a percentage of GNP can be accounted for by levels of societal stress and political instability.

In the process of building political unity, a nation may acquire aggressive tendencies as the leadership uses military preparedness, fear of invasion, pride in national prestige, and expansionist sentiments to build national solidarity (Wright, 1964: 213).

PROPOSITION 19:   *There is a moderate relationship between domestic political factors and a nation's voting in, and support of, the U.N.*

Two studies try to relate political variables to particular dimensions of U.N. voting. Alker and Russett (1965: 237) analyze voting in the General Assembly sessions of 1947, 1952, 1957, and 1961 and find that the degree of political competitiveness is related to the "self-determination" dimension of U.N. voting. Vincent uses the factor analyses of Alker and Russett (1965) and Russett (1966) in a cross-sectional study of voting in the 1960s. His finding (1971: 489-490) is that the factor of "instability" accounts for eight percent of the variance in the "U.N. intervention" dimension of voting, and that the factor of "voting intensity" accounts for five percent of the variance in the "Iberia" dimension.

The percentage of the variance in voting accounted for by these political variables is low, and hence the term "moderate" in Proposition 19. The proposition is further weakened by the following: major changes in regime or other developments have had little impact on voting alignment in the U.N., with the exception of a society-shattering revolution (Cuba) and political changes in several other states (Guatemala, Iran). This finding, based on U.N. voting in 1957-1958 and 1963-1964, is reported in Russett (1967:91). Although major shifts in alignment may not occur, nevertheless states may be sensitive to domestic influences in individual votes:

Regimes faced with strong internal opposition, particularly if this opposition is free to express itself, to mobilize a mass base, and to challenge the government periodically at elections, are much more likely than "representatives" from non-competitive states to be sensitive to socio-economic influences [in their U.N. votes] " (Alker and Russett, 1965: 268).

PROPOSITION 20:   *There is a negative relationship between a nation's political development and its support for international law and organizations.*

Based on an analysis of "major" and "controversial" roll-call votes in the Sixth (Legal) Committee of the U.N. between 1952 and 1966, it has been found that indicators of political development are negatively related to a change orientation in international law (Todd, 1971: 311). A reason for this negative relationship is suggested by Rubinstein, though his analysis focuses on support for economic inter-governmental organizations rather than for international law. Looking at the United States and the Soviet Union only, Rubinstein (1964: 50-51) finds that pressing domestic concerns give rise to a number of similarities in Soviet and American behavior; both are opposed to any expansion of the responsibilities of these organizations, both are concerned with gaining parliamentary victories, and both oppose any new programs which they believe they cannot dominate. For domestic political reasons, then, advanced societies tend not to support international organizations; by extension they do not support an expansion of international law, but this is not tested in the Rubinstein article.

PROPOSITION 21: *Variations in the domestic politics of a nation over time are related to its international inter-actions.*

Several studies lend support to this proposition; but since they all operationalize their variables in different ways, they can hardly be compared and so will simply be listed here. Rummel (1969: 234) finds that "the international politics of a nation as represented by bloc allegiance, bloc trade, U.S. and U.S.S.R. aid, and U.N. votes in agreement with the U.S. and U.S.S.R., are closely related to its political orientation."

In an analysis of "Western Europe" (all states not members of the Warsaw Pact plus non-European NATO countries), Arosalo (1970: 254) reports that interaction in the different types of international nongovernmental organizations tend to be higher for countries of high political participation, with the exception that interaction in international business organizations tends to be higher for countries of low political participation. Also dealing with organizations, Haas (1965: xxxiii) finds that the European Coal and Steel Community gained acceptance in those states which were fragmented ideologically and socially. Finally, Smoker (1965: 167) finds that political events are related to trade for the superpowers in the period 1948-1962: "while it is possible that changes in defence expenditure cause changes in the trade ratio, it seems more likely that, for the United States and the Soviet Union, the two are both subject to a common fluctuation, and a common lag relative to political events."

Cobb and Elder tend to disconfirm the proposition in an analysis of 1176 pairs of nations in the global system of 1955, but we cannot be sure since the variables are different. Using two different aspects of domestic politics, they find (1970: 135) only a slight relationship between the political homogeneity of nations, measured in terms of affective and policy components, and what Cobb and Elder call the "mutual relevance" of each member of a pair for the other. And they find (1970: 135) that "the relative stability of political regimes of two nations and their average duration has little relation to patterns of mutual intercourse in the global system."

PROPOSITION 22:   *Domestic politics affect the success of an interventionist foreign policy.*

We divide this proposition into two subsets: the effect of the domestic politics of the actor on the success of its acts, and the effect of the domestic politics of the target nation on the success of acts directed at it. No quantitative studies on the subject have been done, but there are a number of comparative case studies to examine.

The success of intervention to bring about social change in the five cases studied by Ness (1969: 60-62) was associated with the existence of general and undifferentiated support for reform in the interventionist nation, a very specific reform orientation in certain decision-makers capable of having an impact on the host society, and the pressure of homogeneous interest groups urging decision-makers to act. Intervention of a different kind was studied by Brzezinski and Huntington (1963: 382-388), who find that the success of the U.S.S.R. in Hungary and the failure of the U.S. in

Cuba in 1961 were due in part to political ideology—in terms of justification of the use of force, ability to adapt to change, criteria for estimating what external actions will be tolerated—and to the nature of the political system—in terms of the secrecy with which plans can be formulated and the necessity to be responsive to political pressure. A third type of intervention that has been studied is the pressure of belligerents on neutral nations to join their side. Fox (1959: 184) reports that the success of this type of pressure is associated with the following political variables: the degree of political unity, the moral inhibition against the use of force when there is an alternative, and the groups identifying themselves with the small state.

We turn now to the second subset of this proposition. Ness (1969: 60-62) finds that there are two political variables in the target nation that affect the success of acts designed to bring about social change. One is the existence of general forces for reform that have arisen from the general characteristics of the society, and the other is the existence of clear-cut targets or symbols for reform around which mass support can be mobilized. McKenna (1962: 201) finds that domestic politics in the target nation of the five American diplomatic protests he studied affects the success of these protests. But he does not find a relationship between effective domestic control in the target nation and the success of these acts.

PROPOSITION 23:   *There is a negative relationship between the domestic security of elites and the instability of the international system.*

Two studies directly contradict each other with respect to this proposition. The difference between the two works may be a function of the difference in nations studied and the time period—one focuses on nine different stages of the international system between 1740 and 1960, and the other focuses only on France and China in the post-World War II period. It may also be a function of the dependent variable used—one looks at general international instability, and the other looks at the instability within a bloc. Holsti and Sullivan (1969: 154), in the more limited research, find a negative relationship: only leaders secure from internal dissent adopt policies that violate important bloc norms, thus leading to instability within the bloc. Rosecrance (1963: 304), in his broad historical overview, finds that international instability goes up as domestic insecurity goes up.

PROPOSITION 24:   *The degree of support by domestic interest groups is positively related to the success of a policy of international unification.*

The activities of pressure groups have largely been ignored in comparative studies of foreign policy. The work of Ernst Haas (1968: xxxiii-xxxiv) on the European Coal and Steel Community contains the only findings relevant to this proposition. Haas finds that interest groups support or oppose an international unification scheme on the basis of a calculation of advantage and not on the basis of "ideals" of integration. If the capabilities of an international authority for solving problems are greater than those of a member state's government, then the groups support the former, and their activity adds to the various sources of the integrative impulse. The reason that the European Coal and Steel Community was widely accepted at the beginning was simply that it offered many advantages to many groups. And the process of acceptance was eased because there was "a tradition, however vague, of mutual consultation and of rudimentary value sharing."

Once established, the central authority contributes to true political integration only if it adopts policies consistent with the demands of the interest groups. In this process, the groups organize across national boundaries in order to exert influence on the national foreign policy-making process, and in this way, integration is achieved. Temporary setbacks may not turn the groups against the central authority; on the contrary, they may spur the groups into more intense activity, thus integrating themselves even further into organizations of a cross-national character.

Miscellaneous Findings

The level of conflict behavior has been correlated in many studies with domestic politics. However, only one study examines the effect of domestic violence on the frequency of cooperation. East and Gregg (1967: 266) find these two variables unrelated in their study of 82 nations.

Legvold (1970: 331-344) reports the following in an analysis of Soviet foreign policy for the years 1959 to 1968: the decline of revolutionary potentialities in six West African nations, especially in Guinea, Ghana, and Mali, shifted the nature of Soviet foreign policy objectives in Africa. Whereas around 1960 the Soviets focused on a few West African countries in hopes of spreading socialism, countering the influence of China, and gaining short-term benefits in the Cold War, by 1968 the Soviets were focusing on the important countries throughout the continent in hopes that their regimes, whether socialist or not, would be favorable to Soviet positions in international politics.

Finally, we can look at a study which uses political party ideology as the independent variable. In a diachronic analysis of the British Labour Party between 1914 and 1965, Gordon (1969: 285) finds that the party's commitment to a distinctive doctrine of international politics accounts for the recurrent crises in its foreign policy preferences.

Evaluation

If the hypotheses formulated by political scientists were all tested as extensively as those in Proposition 15, 16, and 17, the discipline would be in better shape today. The research on these three propositions provide an excellent illustration of the way social science should be done. Rummel first tested the hypothesis for his set of nations, using the variables "domestic conflict" and "foreign conflict" and with no time lag. Tanter then replicated his study, adding two variations: he examined another time period and he lagged his correlations. Weede and East and Gregg also did replications, and expanded the generality of the hypotheses by producing the same results with different time periods and numbers of nations. The next step was to break the variables down into types: Collins examined the proposition for different types of foreign conflict within Africa; Haas used different types of domestic conflict; and Gregg and Banks broke down both variables. The question was then examined by Wilkenfeld, who categorized types of nations as well as types of conflict. Wilkenfeld then completed the replicative process by introducing time lags of plus and minus one and two years, and by joining with Zinnes to examine the effect of domestic politics on the transition probabilities from one level of foreign conflict to another.

Substantively, the results of this replication are interesting. Rummel's work, aggregated at a high level, produced the finding that there was no relationship at all between the two variables. Wilkenfeld, when he disaggregated the variables and the sample of nations, found that the relationship between the variables depended on the type of nation and type of conflict considered. We thus have a good illustration of the dangers of doing research at too high a level of abstraction and the importance of "issues" in the analysis of foreign policy.

Unfortunately, the other propositions in this section are not so well tested. Particularly disappointing is the noncomparability of the findings. Many studies have been done correlating some aspect of domestic politics to some aspect of the foreign policy. However, the studies are so disparate that we cannot claim to have much cumulative knowledge on the subject.

The most conspicuous gaps in the literature on political variables concern pressure groups and the political party system. Except for a few comparative case studies (Haas,

Clemens, Bunker), pressure groups are ignored in studies of foreign policy. Except for the work of McGowan, the party system is also ignored as a factor. In addition, we would like to see research in the near future on those propositions where the findings appear to directly contradict one another.

Chapter VII

GOVERNMENTAL VARIABLES

The separation of governmental from political variables does not suggest that the factors considered in this section are not "political." The division was made simply to distinguish the dynamic political processes from the more static or "structural" attributes of the "nation as a whole." These include such things as the form of government, military power, and length of independence. The section also includes findings that postulate that several independent variables, "taken together," influence foreign policy output: these findings, since they could not be broken down and parcelled out to other chapters in the *Survey* are included here under the independent variable "national attributes."

PROPOSITION 25: *The type of government a nation has is reflected in its foreign policy formulation process.*

One way to classify governments is to divide them into presidential, parliamentary, and authoritarian systems. In a comparative case study, Waltz (1967: 307) finds that "in matters of foreign policy (and domestic policy as well) the American Presidential system is superior to British Parliamentary government." He also concludes (1967: 308) that in the conduct of foreign policy "democratic governments of the Western type are well able to compete with authoritarian states."

Related to this classification is the method of dividing states according to the degree of accountability to their citizens: nations are called "open" or "closed" as they are more or less attentive to the demands of the population. Two studies try to account for foreign policy using this variable, and they contradict one another. In research using factor analysis on 119 nations for 1963, Moore (1970: 75) finds that accountability is one of the three most important variables associated with foreign policy behavior. Salmore and Hermann (1969: 23), in a regression analysis of 76 nations for 1966 and 1967, report that accountability explains little of the variance in foreign policy behavior.

Another method of classifying governments focuses on the degree of development of political structures. The Benjamin and Edinger study (1971: 14) on Germany, France, Japan, and the United States reports that political structure is one of six variable groups that show a small to moderate positive relationship with military control of foreign policy. But although we can find a relationship between structural development and the general process of policy-making, we have not been able to connect this variable to specific outputs. For 115 polities in 1963, there is no correlation between violent and diplomatic foreign conflict and access to political channels, differentiation of political institutions, sectionalism within developing systems, kind of legitimation, and type of interest circulation (Gregg and Banks, 1965: 614).

PROPOSITION 26:   *There is no correlation between the degree of democracy or autocracy and the violent foreign conflict behavior of a state.*

Rummel (1968: 204-213) supports this proposition in his study of 77 nations for 1955-1957. Using the same (DON) data but for a longer time period, 1955-1960, Weede (1970: 234) also finds no relationship for 59 nations. And Wright (1964: 161), in his study of wars in history, comes to the same conclusion. But Wright does present some findings which modify the proposition. He reports (1964: 158-159) that "constitutionalism is more favorable to peace than is absolutism" and that the changes in governments from autocracy to democracy are associated with involvement in war.

PROPOSITION 27: *There is a positive relationship between the military power of a state and its foreign conflict behavior.*

If one is to make policy prescriptions, one must be able to predict the consequences of a suggested policy, and these predictions must be based on empirical findings. Proposition 27 is an excellent example of this process. The proposition raises a host of normative questions, among them the effects of arms sales on the recipients' conflict behavior and the effects of arms races on world peace. The positive findings reported provide answers to these questions and can form the basis of policy analysis.

Two very broad research projects support this proposition. Wright's (1964: 167-168) study of wars in modern history reports a positive correlation between the relative power of a state and its warlikeness. The Correlates of War Project on wars between 1816 and 1965 has produced the following results: the major powers have been the most likely nations to engage in war during this period (Small and Singer, 1970: 151). The level of power capability and diplomatic importance and the rates of change in these variables together account for 72 percent of the variance in the amount of war begun in each half-decade of the period (Singer, 1972: 267). A high concentration in the major powers' capabilities, changes in this concentration, and the rate of capability distribution together account for 73 percent of the variance in nineteenth century war and 35 percent of the variance in twentieth century war.

Two other studies also look at a large number of nations, but for more limited time periods. Both of them look at several types of conflict behavior besides war. Operationalizing the independent variable as "military preparedness" for 84 nations in the period 1955 to 1961, the Feierabends (1969: 150-151) find a positive correlation with foreign conflict only for the "high modern" nations. Keim (1971: 289-290) examines about 100 nations for 1963 in terms of conflict "uniqueness," a measure based on the distance of a nation from others on five dimensions of conflict behavior from the DON Project. He finds that nations with more unique conflict patterns are those with higher total military expenditures (tau = .419), higher military expenditure as a percentage of GNP (tau = .295), and a higher percentage of the population in the armed forces (tau = .263).

Finally, two studies examine specific conflicts, and their findings also support Proposition 27. Choucri and North (1969: 56) discover a high positive correlation between defense allocations and international violence involving the members of the Triple Entente and Triple Alliance between 1870 and 1914. Conversely, one would expect small defense allocations to be associated with low levels of violence: Touval (1966: 647) finds that the lack of military capability of Morocco and Somalia contributed to the containment of the border disputes in which they were involved in the 1960s.

Military power has been correlated with other types of conflict besides violent conflict. Weede (1970: 230) finds that "powerful states tend to engage in much more verbal foreign conflict activity than powerless states." And Chadwick (1969: 200) finds, in an analysis of 64 nations using the DON data for 1955, that "nations with large force capabilities tend to engage in more diplomatic conflict than do nations with smaller force capabilities."

A possible explanation for all of these findings is offered in the Benjamin and Edinger study (1971: 18). They report that when there is a large military organization and a relatively large part of the GNP devoted to military purposes, the military is likely to be a significant influence in foreign policy formation.

Rummel (1968: 204-213) contradicts Proposition 27, finding little relationship between national power and foreign conflict behavior for 77 nations from 1955 to 1957. Weede uses the same data on 59 nations, but he does not transform the data to pull in extreme values. The result is that he finds (1970: 230) an inverse relationship: controlling for verbal conflict, the more powerful states tend to be involved in *less* violent conflict activity.

Two further studies provide a possible resolution of the contradictory studies. Russett controls for level of military capability in his analysis of violent conflict from 1946 to 1965, and he states (1967: 202),

When capabilities—and hence the mutual salience of two countries—are very low, violent conflict is likely to be absent. When capabilities and salience are moderate and narrowly focused, conflict may be quite common. But when capabilities are numerous and varied, the relationship is seldom marked by violence.

Richardson controlled for the type of power used and reported (1960: xii) that "in proportion to their possible contacts for war-making, sea powers seem to have been less belligerent than land powers."

PROPOSITION 28:   *A nation's length of independence is not related to its foreign conflict behavior.*

The research by Keim reported in the previous proposition was designed to test the theory that a nation is gradually socialized into conflict uniqueness as its length of membership in the international system grows. No support was found for the theory: the length of independence of a nation is not related to its conflict uniqueness (Keim, 1971: 290).

If one looks just at war proneness, however, a relationship

does emerge. Wright (1964: 163) finds that the older a state, the more warlike it tends to be.

PROPOSITION 29: *There is little or no relationship between various national attributes, taken together, and a state' foreign conflict and cooperative behavior.*

Rosenau suggests a typology of nations that can be used to analyze foreign policy.[1] It classifies nations according to their size (large and small), wealth (rich and poor), and accountability of political system (open and closed). Using the WEIS data for 1966 and 1967, Salmore and Hermann (1969: 23-29) investigated the extent to which these variables account for the variance in the foreign policy outputs of 76 nations. They find that these three national attributes, taken together, are only weakly related to cooperative and conflictual behavior. They report that size explains more of the variance than the other two until they control for the total number of acts a country initiates, in which case they find that accountability and wealth are better predictors of foreign policy behavior.

Rummel also supports the proposition (1969: 235) that "The foreign conflict behavior of a nation is statistically independent of its economic development, size, political system, density, and Catholic culture." But when he analyzes conflict dyadically, relationships appear. For 40 dyads in 1955-1957 he finds (1966a: 144) that "the magnitude of foreign conflict between nations is a resultant of the forces of their distances on dimensions of wealth, power (joint power), geographic distance, and value." For 182 dyads in 1955, he finds (1969: 238) that "the more similar two nations are in economic development, political orientation, Catholic culture, and density, . . . the less conflictful their interaction will be." And "the more dissimilar two nations are in economic development and size and the greater their joint technological capability to span geographic distance is, the more overt conflict they have with each other." (1969: 238).

Haas (1968b: 109) looks at a different set of national

attributes and contradicts Proposition 29. Obviously then, we need separate propositions for different attributes, but sufficient research to warrant this is not yet available. Haas' study, focusing on the period 1955-1960, concludes that an asymmetrical pattern of national attributes is three times as likely to be associated with aggression as a symmetrical pattern; these attributes include resources, demotypes (aggregated human elements), attitudes, behaviors, functions, and structures.

Finally, East and Gregg (1967: 265), using the DON data for 82 nations, find that those national attributes which are positively correlated to conflict behavior are also positively correlated to cooperative behavior. There are some exceptions: the variables of government control of the press, equality of land distribution, voting with the United States in the United Nations, and a large number of neighboring states show different correlations with the two types of foreign policy output.

PROPOSITION 30: *If the military-strategic balance favors one nation in a dispute, the conflict will tend not to escalate.*

A key factor in containing the eight crises studied by Schwartz (1967: 486) was the possession by the United States of "strong, clearly superior strategic forces, the capacity to bring these forces to bear in a crisis, the resolve to do so, and the ability to communicate these matters to Soviet decision makers." Similarly, Russett (1963: 109) reports that, in the seven instances in which deterrence was successful and the cirsis contained, one of the properties present was that the defender had overall strategic superiority. Wright (1965: 441-442) also confirms the proposition: the greater and the more obvious the inequality of force between nations and the greater the capability for destruction, the smaller the chance that a conflict will escalate. However, if leaders do not, at the time the crisis is initiated, have superior forces, but believe they will have them in the future, then the conflict will escalate (Wright, 1965: 441-442).

PROPOSITION 31: *There is a relationship between various govern-mental variables and a nation's voting position in, and support of, the United Nations.*

The degree of democracy is related to several dimensions of U.N. voting. Alker and Russett (1965: 225-228) and Alker (1964: 654-655) find that it is related to the "East versus West" dimension of voting. The latter study is based on 70 nonunanimous, nonprocedural roll calls in the committees and plenary sessions of the sixteenth General Assembly, while the former is based on a varying number of votes in the sessions of 1947, 1952, 1957, and 1961. Alker and Russett's analysis also finds degrees of democracy to be related to the "Palestine-related" dimension of voting. Vincent uses the Alker and Russett data in a cross-sectional study of voting in the 1960s, and finds (1971: 486-490) that the factor of "democracy" accounts for 34 percent, 5 percent and 4 percent of the variance in the "Eastern voting," "Southern voting," and "Iberia" dimensions respectively. Finally, taking a somewhat different approach, Alker (1969: 706) notes that in 52 roll call votes distributed over eight sessions of the General Assembly (1947-1963), communist states have tended to be antisupranationalistic.

The number of years an African nation has been indepen-dent and its per capita defense expenditures were both found to be related to the degree to which it voted with other African nations during the 1960-1961 session (Ellis and Salzberg, 1965: 31). And the first of these two variables shows a significant positive correlation (for 101 members in 1963) to the "economic factor of U.N. support and a significant negative correlation to the "system-change" factor of U.N. support for all nations and for the less developed nations (Clark, O'Leary, and Wittkopf, 1971: 20-21). In addition, these authors find that the degree of internal freedom of a nation shows a positive correlation to the system-change and economic factors of support for all nations and to the system-change factor for the developed nations.

PROPOSITION 32: *There is a positive relationship between a govern-ment's power and its success at the United Nations.*

The question of whether more powerful nations get elected to U.N. office more frequently than others is dealt with in two works. A positive relationship is found in both analyses, but only for regional groups of nations. Examining the activity of twenty Latin American states between 1945 and 1963, Gregg (1965: 153) finds that

the correlation between power and frequency of election has been most conspicuous in elections to the Security Council, and the presidency of the General Assembly . . . and least conspicuous in election to the Trusteeship Council and the main committee offices.

For 25 African nations between 1961 and 1965, Weigart and Riggs (1969: 12) find a positive correlation between economic and military capability and U.N. office-holding. ·

Stoessinger studies success in the U.N. also, not in terms of office-holding, but in terms of furthering a nation's policies. He reports (1970: 176) that the United States has been more successful than the U.S.S.R. in manipulating the U.N. to further its foreign policies because the United States has more allies in all U.N. organs, contributes a larger share to the budgets of the organization, and is more experienced in working in a parliamentary framework.

PROPOSITION 33: *There is a relationship between national attri-butes and international interaction.*

Ideally we would list separate propositions for each type of national attribute and each type of interaction, unless research allowed us to be more general. But we have been forced to state this proposition vaguely because the several studies are not comparable; no effort has been made to produce cumulative general knowledge.

In the broadest study included here, McGowan (1968: 290) analyzes political, economic, and military interaction for 32 African nations for the period 1963-1965, and finds that closed societies are high interactors and open societies are low interactors. Chadwick (1969: 205) examines inter-action through alliances for 64 nations in 1955 and finds that "nations with large force capabilities tend to enter into alliances more frequently than nations with small force capabilities."

Brams (1966: 889) observes that from 1962 to 1964 the dyads among communist nations formed quite private sub-groups in trade, diplomatic exchanges, and shared IGO memberships, although to a greater extent on the latter than on the other two. East reports (1969: 127) that, among 115 nations analyzed for the periods 1950-1964 and 1960-1961, "highly mobile states tend to join more IGO's over time, are involved in less international conflict, and have lower scores on a general measure of participation in international politics." Vellut (1967: 266) finds that the very small African states are unable to interact in the international system and play the shock-absorbing role that maintains international equilibrium.

Very little work has been done on the interaction between nations in negotiation. In a study of 22 rounds of the U.S.-U.S.S.R. disarmament negotiations between 1946 and 1960, Jensen (1965: 163) finds an inverse relationship between military strength and bargaining. When the two nations are highly confident about their deterrent capabili-ties, the incentives for serious consideration of disarmament are negligible, and so they make few concessions.

PROPOSITION 34: *The greater a nation's power, the more successful it is in foreign policy.*

Generally it has been true that military power leads to military success; the major powers have been the most successful in war in terms of a won-lost record (Small and Singer, 1970: 153). Looking not at war but at coercive diplomacy, George et al. (1971: 216) report that military power is not the only ingredient to success. The existence of usable military options is a necessary but not sufficient condition of success in U.S. coercive diplomacy; it was present in the case of failure as well as in the case of success.

Military strength is not the only measure of a nation's power, and, of course, military success is not the only kind of foreign policy success. In her analysis of five neutral nations in World War II, Fox (1959: 184-185) concludes that the following internal conditions increased the would-be neutral's chances of successfully resisting pressures from the belligerents: capacity to forcefully resist an act of violence, a conciliatory approach when necessary, unity in the government and in the populace, friendly relations with neighboring small states, concentration on the main goal to the exclusion of others, accurate military intelligence about the belligerents, skillful negotiators, the ability to play one side against the other and so extract from both concessions and support, the ability to hold out and avoid a decision until its timeliness disappears, and a history of negotiation with the great powers. McKenna (1962: 199-200) correlates two governmental variables to the success of five U.S. diplomatic protests. He finds no relationship between the capacity for action and the success of the protest, but he does find that protests directed at great powers will not be successful as often as those directed at small powers.

Miscellaneous Findings

Holsti and Sullivan (1969: 158) draw the following conclusion based on a study of France and China since World War II:

Nonconforming alliance policy of an open polity tends to remain confined to a few issue-areas; that is, there is little tendency for disputes to "spill over" into all issue areas. Nonconforming alliance policy of a closed polity tends to spill over into all issue-areas.

Clemens (1966: 61) finds that the trends of Soviet diplomacy and propaganda on arms control between 1954 and 1964 are related to the military-strategic situation.

Finlay, Holsti, and Fagen—on the basis of an analysis of Nkrumah and other Ghanaian leaders, Dulles, and Castro—make this statement (1967: 235):

greatest leadership impact [in the use of foreign enemies in international politics] is possible in those rapidly changing political systems characterized by authoritarian forms of rule and little or no institutionalization of top roles.

Evaluation

The reader has probably noticed that the independent variable in many of the propositions of this section is "government variables" or "national attributes;" in only a few propositions have we used more specific terms like "degree of democracy" or "military power." The reason for this is simply that the research is so diverse that, in order to organize findings into propositions, we have had to be very general. Ideally, each proposition should employ one specific independent variable; until there is greater theoretical agreement about basic concepts and their measures and more replication to enable us to build such propositions, we are forced to compare studies at this very general level.

In view of the degree to which the cold war has sparked government investment in research, it is surprising that there are not more studies like Waltz's and those in Proposition 25 that try to compare the foreign policy behavior of democratic and autocratic states. Also, in view of the numerous typologies of systems that have been developed in the field of comparative politics, which has grown so rapidly since World War II, it is surprising that there is no empirical work that tries to relate political system-type to foreign policy output. For instance, can the typologies developed by Apter or Almond be operationalized and used in the comparative study of foreign policy? Should they be used in this way?

There are many competent studies in this section, but the very small amount of replication forces us to withhold judgment on their validity. Even in Proposition 27, where a number of findings all point in a confirming direction, the diversity of the variables used limits our confidence. Until each of those variables is placed in a separate proposition, which is then confirmed by several studies, the usefulness of the research surveyed here will remain limited.

NOTE

1. James N. Rosenau, "Pre-Theories and Theories of Foreign Policy," pp. 27-93 in R. B. Farrell (ed.) *Approaches to Comparative and International Politics* (Evanston, Ill.: Northwestern University Press, 1966).

Chapter VIII

ECONOMIC VARIABLES

While the Marxist notion that economic phenomena underlie all foreign policy has generally been discredited, it is nonetheless valid to consider economic variables as one of the correlates of a nation's behavior in the international system. In this section we examine the influence of such factors as level of economic development, amount of trade, balance of payments, and nature of the economy.

PROPOSITION 35: *The level of a nation's economic development affects the formulation of its foreign policy.*

The only statistical analysis that supports this proposition is McGowan's study of 45 nations in the 1960s. His conclusion (1970: 203) is that nations of greater societal wealth will experience more conflict in foreign policy formation. Three comparative case studies also confirm the proposition. Bandyopadhyaya (1968: 33) finds that economic development is a major influence on the foreign policy of India and Pakistan, but at a diminishing rate over time. Bunker (1969: 296) comes to essentially the same conclusion for Peru in a diachronic analysis of the period 1958 to 1966. Clemens (1966: 63) also finds a relationship between the two variables; but in his particular case of Soviet arms control policy, he finds economic pressures only a marginal, and not determining, factor in foreign policy formulation.

In order to determine the effect of economic development on who controls the formulation of foreign policy, we must again turn to the Benjamin and Edinger study (1971: 18-19). They report that the lower the GNP, the more likely it is that the military will control foreign policy-making. But this does not imply that poor countries will have high levels of foreign conflict behavior. As we shall see in Proposition 37, there is no relationship between economic development and foreign conflict.

PROPOSITION 36: *The more economically developed a nation is, the greater is its level of activity in the international system.*

For 82 nations, Rummel (1969: 234) finds that economic development is one of the two major factors (the other being size) accounting for the activity of nations: "The more economically developed and larger a nation is, the more it will be active in the international system." Moore's study (1970: 75) of 119 nations in 1963 supports Rummel, but Salmore and Hermann (1969: 23) contradict these two, finding that economic development does not explain much of the variance in the activities of 76 states during 1966 and 1967.

McGowan (1969: 217-218) supports Proposition 36 using a different approach. He tries to categorize the types of foreign policy activity of 30 African nations for 1963 and 1964. The results of his analysis are that states with the highest levels of economic development tend to be "active-independent" states, those with intermediate levels of development tend to be "transitional" states, and those with low levels of development tend to be "inactive-dependent" states.

PROPOSITION 37: *There is no relationship between the level of economic development and a nation's foreign conflict behavior.*

Rummel's study (1968: 204-213) of 77 nations for the period 1955-1957 and his study (1967b: 197) of 82 nations for 1955 operationalize the variables in this proposition using the DON data and find no relationship between them. In a replication for 82 nations, East and Gregg (1967: 266) find that economic development is not related to conflict or cooperation. Richardson (1960: xi) measures conflict in terms of deadly quarrels and finds no correlation between economic development and 300 deadly quarrels between 1820 and 1945. Finally, Choucri and North (1969:56) support the proposition in their analysis of the members of the Triple Entente and Triple Alliance between 1870 and 1914.

Haas (1965: 323) contradicts these studies in his analysis of about 70 nations: "Rich countries have more foreign conflict than more of the economically developing nations of the world." The Feierabends break down 84 nations into types and find (1969: 150-151), for the years 1955-1961, that economic development is positively related to foreign conflict for "high modern" nations and negatively related for "mid-modern" nations.

PROPOSITION 38: *The type of economic system and other economic variables affect a nation's involvement in war.*

Wright categorizes economic systems in two ways. Looking at the socialism-capitalism continuum, he finds (1964: 302, 305) that capitalist societies have been among the most peaceful, and socialist societies among the most warlike, of all societies. Looking at the economic base of the society, he concludes (1964: 165): "States with economics based on agriculture, though less warlike than those based on animal pasturage, have generally been more warlike than those based on commerce and industry."

Using other economic characteristics, Fox's study (1959: 184) of five neutrals in World War II reveals that the more self-contained the neutral state's economy, the better are its chances of resisting the pressures from belligerents and staying out of war. The Feierabends (1969: 150-151) find an inverse relationship between foreign trade as a percentage of GNP and foreign conflict, but only for the "low modern" group of nations.

The economic capacity of a nation to sustain military activities is a major determinant of its tendencies to become involved in war. Research has supported this hypothesis on a general scale and in specific disputes. In a study of 45 conflicts in the twentieth century, Wright (1965: 441-442) finds that the higher the cost of conflict in proportion to the state's economy, the smaller the chance is that the conflict will escalate. This factor of economic capacity was the reason that seven border disputes in Africa in the 1960s remained at low levels of conflict (Touval, 1966: 647). And thus can we understand the course of the arms race in the Middle East: because the growth rate of Israel's economy was higher than Egypt's, Syria's, or Iraq's, Israel was gradually able to win the arms race in the 1953-1965 period (Lambelet, 1971: 166).

Although a relationship between economic variables and war has been established in these studies, Richardson (1960: xi) finds that the relationship is a moderate one at best; and that territorial disputes, which he considered more political than economic, are a more important factor in causing wars. Richardson's conclusion (1960b: xi) is this:

Economic causes seem to have figured directly in less than 29 percent of the wars. Among such causes taxation of colonials and minorities; economic assistance to an enemy; restrictions on movements of capital, trade, and migration; and dissatisfaction of soldiers have had an influence, the importance of which has been approximately in this order.

PROPOSITION 39: *The level of a nation's economic development is a determinant of its voting behavior in the United Nations.*

It is rare that the findings of two authors are so close that they are worded in practically identical manner, and the occasion deserves quotation. Rummel (1969: 234) concludes that "Economic development is the single most important determinant of U.N. voting behavior;" Vincent (1971: 493), that " 'Economic Development' is the most important predictor" of a nation's voting in the U.N. The former study focuses on 82 nations in the General Assembly session of 1955, while the latter covers about 100 nations for the early 1960s. Furthermore, Rummel (1969: 238) finds that the more similar two nations are in their economic development, the more aligned their U.N. voting will be.

Several studies confirm a relationship between economic development and specific dimensions of U.N. voting which have been identified through factor analysis. Alker's (1964) analysis of 70 votes in the sixteenth General Assembly reports that economic development is related to the "self-determination" dimension of voting, and per capita GNP is related to the "North versus South" dimension. Alker and Russett (1965: 225-242) also correlate per capita GNP to the "North versus South" dimension for four different sessions, and also to the "East versus West," "Palestine-related," and "self-determination" dimensions. Vincent's study (1971: 486, 489) mentioned in the last paragraph, finds that the factor of "Economic Development" accounts for 21 percent and 33 percent of the variance in the "eastern voting" and "southern voting" dimensions, respectively.

One more study should be mentioned in connection with this proposition, although both of its variables are different from those used in the other research. Ellis and Salzberg (1965: 31) analyze 100 General Assembly votes of 24 African nations and find that the index of adherence to the voting of other African nations is related to the ratio of a nation's major export to its total exports and the ratio of its exports to its imports. The authors do not, however, explain why this should be the case.

PROPOSITION 40:   *Wealthy nations tend to be elected to United Nations offices more frequently than poor nations.*

Weigart and Riggs (1969: 12) report a positive correlation between economic and social development and U.N. office-holding for the period 1961-1965. Gregg (1965: 151) uses rank in the scale of budget assessment as his independent variable, but this measure reflects national wealth. He studies twenty Latin American states between 1945 and 1963 and comes to the same conclusion that Weigart and Riggs do for African states. Singer and Sensenig (1963: 902) perform a more extensive analysis, covering all U.N. members except the permanent members of the security council. With GNP as the independent variable and the n ranging from 53 to 105 nations, they support the findings of the two regional studies.

PROPOSITION 41:   *The higher are a nation's trade and income levels, the lower is its support for the United Nations.*

The richer nations tend to offer less support for the United Nations. Vincent's study (1968: 928-929) of 68 permanent U.N. delegations in 1968 reveals that if a state is highly developed, the attitudes of its delegates toward the U.N. will be negative and static. Similarly, his study (1970: 142) of nine caucusing groups reveals that delegates from the more developed groups will be less supranationalistic in their attitudes. These attitudes are reflected in contributions to the U.N. budget: the rich nations pay less than their share according to their national incomes (Pincus, 1965: 111). Since the poor nations are often exempt from payments, this leaves the middle-income countries, mostly European, to carry a disproportionate part of the burden. These variables are also reflected in attitudes towards the international legal activities of the U.N. In the Sixth (Legal) Committee of the U.N. between 1952 and 1966, more economically developed nations had a lower "change orientation" toward international law.

The analysis by Clark, O'Leary, and Wittkopf (1971:

20-21) of 101 U.N. members in 1963 finds several correlations between trade and income levels and U.N. support. A nation's total financial resources show a significant negative correlation to the "system-change" factor of support for all nations, and a significant positive correlation to the "system-conforming" and "economic" factors for less developed nations. Per capita GDP shows a significant negative correlation to the "system-change" factor and a significant positive correlation to the "economic" factor for all nations. The foreign trade/GDP ratio shows a significant positive correlation to the "system-change" factor for all nations and for the developed nations.

Does Proposition 41 extend to support for other types of international cooperation and organization besides the U.N.? In research on 17 regional groupings in the mid-1960s, Rittberger (1971: 114) examines three dimensions of cooperation: the international division of labor (intermeshing of national economies through exchange processes or multinational corporations), supranational bureaucracies, and transnational sodalities (defined on page 101 as "cross-national associational linkages among nationally organized groups whose members occupy comparable roles in their respective national societies"). Generally Rittberger finds no relationships, negative or positive, between aspects of industrial civilization and the dimensions of international cooperation. He does report, however, that "among regions of underdeveloped countries, those who suffer from the greatest backwardness are most inclined to strengthen organized multinational cooperation (except for transnational sodalities);" this finding is consistent with others reported in Proposition 41.

PROPOSITION 42:   *The greater the economic development of a country, the greater is the level of its interactions in the international system.*

McGowan (1968: 290) measures interaction for 32 African states between 1963 and 1965 along political, economic, and military dimensions. He finds that the more highly developed states are high interactors and the less developed are low interactors; also, those states that have dependent economies (single product and/or single main customer) tend to be low interactors. The relationship holds for a broader spectrum of nations, at least in two specific kinds of interaction. For about 100 nations in the 1960s, there is a strong relationship between the level of a country's development and the size of its overseas diplomatic establishment (O'Leary, 1969: 338). For 96 nations in 1962, there is a moderately strong relationship between GNP per capita and the interaction of delegates in the U.N.'s Fifth Committee, rho = .53 (Alger, 1968).

The Feierabends (1969: 154) develop a typology of interactive behavior, but their research on 84 nations between 1955 and 1961 produces disappointing results in terms of our proposition. The "feuding" posture is related to the mid-modern countries, but the other three types of interactive postures—"high participant," "withdrawal," and "supportive"—cannot be tied to a particular level of development.

PROPOSITION 43: *There is a relationship between a nation's economic conditions and its level of trade and aid ties.*

Pincus (1965: 187) reports that as a nation grows economically, its trade will also increase. This may be true in absolute figures, but relative to income, a nation's trade may drop as development proceeds. Deutsch and Eckstein (1961: 22-286) find that for fourteen Western nations plus Japan between 1890 and 1959, this was indeed the case—that the ratio of foreign trade to national income decreased as industrialization progressed. In a study of 73 nations for 1955, it was found that there is a further decrease in the ratio of foreign trade to national income as per capita GNP increased (Deutsch, Bliss, and Eckstein, 1962: 365). Finally, trade is little affected by the specialization of a country in specific commodities or by complementarity of resources between two countries. This latter finding is reported by Deutsch (1960b: 48) in a study of 106 nations for 1938 and 1954 and 15 North Atlantic nations for 1890, 1913, 1938, and 1954.

Two more studies correlate economic conditions with trade and aid ties. Vellut's study (1967: 263) of African states reports that factors such as levels or changes in income, the absorptive capacity of the local economy, and capital-output ratio affect the inflow of foreign capital. Walters' (1970: 238) comparison of Soviet and American trade and aid since the second World War concludes that "the basic strength of the American economy gives the United States a significant advantage relative to the Soviet Union in the forging of economic ties to the less developed countries through trade and aid mechanisms."

PROPOSITION 44:   *The greater a nation's trade, the more ties of other kinds it will have with other nations.*

A nation which imports a great deal is more prone to enter into economic/cultural agreements; the relationship is even stronger if the nation exports a good deal (Chadwick, 1969: 205). Also, higher trade levels will strengthen the relationship between military agreements and economic/cultural agreements. Chadwick turns the variables around in his analysis (1969: 205) and finds that a high level of economic/cultural agreements will strengthen the relationship between imports and exports.

Alger and Brams (1967: 660) find that among 119 nations (1963-1964), trade ties showed a strong correlation to the number of diplomats sent and received. Rummel (1969: 238) finds a relationship between export patterns and inter-action in terms of treaties, mail, tourists, emigrants, and student migrations. He notes that the relationship is stronger for nations in overt conflict with each other than for nations without such conflict.

Miscellaneous Findings

In his analysis of five American protests, McKenna (1962: 201) reports that "a correlation of sorts appeared between disparity of basic resources, enormously favorable to the United States, and successful diplomatic action."

Hanrieder's research on Germany's relations with other nations from 1949 to 1963 produced very interesting findings, but no other studies have dealt with the question of penetration. His finding (1967: 234) relevant to this section of the survey is that German preoccupation with domestic economic welfare was one of the factors facilitating penetration of West Germany by the international system.

Evaluation

The contrast between this section and the previous one is striking. Whereas in Chapter VII the independent variables in the propositions were formulated in general terms, here they are more specific variables like economic development, nature of the economy, trade and income levels. Each of these specific propositions has been studied in several works, so that where these works confirm one another, we can say that we have at least the beginnings of knowledge. We have confidence in the following propositions in which a relationship between two specific variables has been found by several authors: 38, 39, 40, 41, and 44.

The effect of economic variables on the formulation of foreign policy (Proposition 35) has been a neglected area of research that future studies should investigate. While conflict behavior has been a prominent dependent variable, cooperative behavior has been studied much less extensively. And the effect of economic variables on the international system—level of tension, degree of bipolarity, nature of international organizations—has been completely ignored in the research literature.

Chapter IX

SOCIETAL VARIABLES

Wars that have arisen over ethnic conflicts or over demands to increase the size of a nation remind us that attributes of the social structure must be considered in research on foreign policy behavior. Thus the comparative study of foreign policy will increasingly require the work of sociologists, just as the work of scholars in other disciplines is required in the previous sections and in the following ones.

PROPOSITION 45: *There is no difference in the relative importance of societal and governmental variables in accounting for foreign policy behavior.*

Moore's analysis of 119 nations tries to determine the relative potency of two independent variables. He dichotomizes nations in three different ways and examines seven foreign policy issues, with the following findings (1970: 60-76). On five of seven issues there is no difference between open and closed nations with respect to the importance of societal and governmental variables. On four of seven issues there is no difference between developed and underdeveloped nations on their relative importance. And on all seven issues there is no difference between large and small nations with respect to societal and governmental influences. However, Moore does find that "societal and governmental variables together tend to be more potent in large than in small nations, where decision-makers appear to be influenced more by external than by internal political linkages."

PROPOSTION 46:   *There is a positive relationship between a nation's size and the general level of its foreign policy activity.*

Using 82 nations as the unit of analysis, Rummel (1969: 234) finds a positive correlation between size and level of activity. And using 164 and 182 dyads as the unit of analysis, he finds (1969: 238) that dissimilarities in size, along with dissimilarities in economic development, account for 85 percent of the variance in the behavior of nations toward each other. Moore (1970: 75) supports Rummel's findings. Salmore and Hermann (1969: 23) offer additional evidence for 76 nations (1966-1967) that size is more strongly related to foreign policy outputs than are wealth or the degree of political accountability.

PROPOSITION 47:   *There is a positive relationship between population size and changes in size and a nation's foreign conflict behavior.*

Whether the explanation is one of *lebensraum* or one of the necessity for adequate manpower and economic resources to engage in foreign adventures, we can expect a positive relationship between the size of a nation and its foreign conflict involvement. The Feierabends' (1969: 150-151) analysis of 84 nations from 1955 to 1961 reports that the size of a country is positively related to foreign conflict for "high modern" and "low modern" nations, and negatively related for "mid-modern" nations. Choucri and North (1969:

47) find that there is a direct path from population size (and technology) to international violence for Britain, Germany, and, to a lesser extent, France between 1870 and 1914. But this relationship between size and war involvement may depend on the type of war one is examining. In the 19th and 20th centuries, the more populous European nations engaged in more continental warfare, but their involvement in extra-continental war was no greater than that of smaller European nations (Singer, 1972: 267). In addition, nations with higher growth rates in population or density are no more war-prone than nations with lower rates (Singer, 1972: 267).

Wright's studies modify these findings. He finds (1964: 293-295) that the pressures of population growth have increased the opportunities for friction but have not often been the direct cause of war. A more important cause than population changes has been the willingness of the people to accept unsound economic theories on the subject. However, *differentials* in rates of population growth, migration, and imperial expansion have resulted in anxieties and conflict through colonial expansion. Those wars that do occur can be classified according to population changes:

imperial wars have been initiated by countries with the most rapidly rising population, whereas balance-of-power wars have been initiated by alliances with the less rapidly rising populations, provided other factors of the military potential are being equally affected by time.

PROPOSITION 48:   *Aspects of the social organization of a nation are related to its foreign conflict behavior.*

Wright's study includes the dynamics of the social structure as an independent variable. He notes (1964: 252): "The organization of greater communities has enlarged the areas and the periods of peace, but at the expense of bigger and worse wars when they have come." Also, socially progressive states tend to be more warlike than more traditional, static states (1964: 166).

The hypothesis that stress precedes international military behavior is not well supported. Countries with high unemployment do go to war very frequently, but not aggressively, and military expenditures are independent of levels of unemployment. Looking more closely at the cases studied, a pattern emerged. In rural countries, war often comes immediately after an unemployment crisis, and inasmuch as the time intervening between the crisis and the outbreak of war is short, there are no large scale military preparations. In urbanized countries, war comes after a period of militarization, which in turn is triggered by an unemployment peak.

Haas continues this study of the relationship between stress and foreign conflict by looking at the frequency of deaths by suicide, homocide, and alcoholism. Generally he finds (1965: 323; 1968a: 243) that there are relationships between these indicators of stress and the military expenditures and war involvement of a nation.

Two studies deny the existence of a relationship between aspects of social organization and foreign policy. East and Gregg (1967: 266) find that the level of ethnic heterogeneity of 82 nations is not associated with foreign conflict or cooperation. Weede's analysis (1970: 234) of 59 nations for the years 1955-1960 concludes that the level of socioeconomic development is not related to verbal or violent foreign conflict.

PROPOSITION 49: *Population losses and changes in the attitudes of people predict the end of war.*

Only three works are relevant to this proposition. Studying survey data on the United States and Great Britain for the periods 1937-1946 and 1950-1953, Campbell and Cain (1965: 319) conclude that the sudden end of war after a long period of persistence and attrition is related to the rapid conversion of the public's attitude from overt hostility and subconscious war-weariness to overt war-weariness and subconscious hositility. (Similarly, they find the outbreak of war to be associated with the rapid change from overt friendship and subconscious hostility to overt hostility and subconscious friendship.) Klingberg (1966: 168) examines the other independent variable mentioned in the proposition in an analysis of eight major wars between 1618 and 1918. His finding is that: "There is some evidence that nations in modern times will tend to surrender before they have suffered population losses greater than three or four percent." Singer (1972: 266) disagrees, finding no "clear battle death threshhold at which the defeated tend to surrender."

PROPOSITION 50: *There is a relationship between population size, density, and composition and a nation's voting in the United Nations.*

Rummel's research (1969: 234, 238) on the foreign policy behavior of 82 nations in 1955 shows that size and density are two of the five factors which account for most of a nation's voting in the United Nations; also, the more similar two nations are in density, the more aligned their U.N. voting will be. In this finding he is backed up by Ellis and Salzberg (1965: 31) who relate the population density of 24 African states to the degree to which each voted with other African states in the 1960-1961 General Assembly session. They do not suggest why this should be so, however.

A series of studies correlate societal variables to particular dimensions of voting. Governments reflected socioeconomic characteristics of their people on "East versus West" and "North versus South" issues in the General Assembly sessions of 1947, 1952, 1957, and 1961 (Alker and Russett, 1965: 268). One of these characteristics was European racial composition (Alker and Russett, 1965: 225-233). Racial variables were also related to voting in the sixteenth General Assembly, specifically on the "North versus South," "self-determination," and "Moslem factor" dimensions of voting (Alker, 1964: 654-655). And in the 1960s, the factor of "bigness" accounted for 13 percent of the variance in the "southern voting" dimension, while "population rate increase" accounted for 10 percent of the variance in the "U.N. intervention" dimension (Vincent, 1971: 489).

PROPOSITION 51: *The greater a nation's population size and density, the greater is its support of the United Nations.*

The research of Clark, O'Leary, and Wittkopf (1971: 20-21) shows significant positive correlations between the population size of 101 members and the "system-conforming" factor of support for all nations, and between population size and the "economic" and "system-conforming" factors of support for the less developed nations. Vincent's work (1968: 928-929) on 68 permanent delegations finds that delegates from nations of low population density have negative and static attitudes toward the U.N.

PROPOSITION 52: *The population size of a nation is related to the level of its interactions with other states.*

All of the studies on this proposition find a relationship between the two variables. There is some question, however, whether the relationship is positive or negative! The answer varies with the particular kind of interaction considered. With more research, we will be able to place each kind of interaction in a separate proposition.

McGowan, for example, finds (1968: 290) a positive relationship between large territory and population and the level of a nation's interactions in terms of political, military, and economic activity. His study covers 32 African states between 1963 and 1965. Deutsch, on the other hand, reports (1960a: 153) a negative correlation between population size and trade interaction for 71 nations in the mid-1950s. This finding is supported by two later studies that Deutsch did with others. One is with Eckstein (1961: 289) and covers 14 Western nations plus Japan, Argentina, and the Soviet Union; the other is an analysis done with Bliss and Eckstein (1962: 363) of 73 nations in 1955. In addition, Deutsch finds (1960a: 151) that population size, along with territory size and per capita number of letters, is also inversely related to interaction in terms of mail flows.

In a well-known study, Cattell (1949: 459) factor analyzed

national attributes for 69 continuously sovereign nations between 1837 and 1937 to produce what he called "dimensions of culture" patterns. His finding relevant to this proposition is that the size of a nation is positively related (factor loading = .33) to the number of secret treaties it enters into. Finally, Alger (1968: 68-69) reports that there is a positive correlation, though a weak one, between population size and the interactions of delegates in the Fifth Committee of the United Nations.

Miscellaneous Findings

There was no proposition with foreign policy formulation as the dependent variable in this section because only one study has related it to societal variables. This is McGowan's research on 45 nations in the 1960s, in which he finds (1970: 199) that "the more differentiated the society, the greater the influence of achievement criteria as a basis of recruitment into foreign policy roles."

Evaluation

The findings reported in this section provide a good illustration of the extent to which research has been guided by the ability to measure phenomena. The societal variables that have been employed in empirical work have centered on the population size of a nation. It is of course much easier to measure size and density than it is to measure variables such as the degree of social stratification, racial conflict, and modernization. Before analysis in this area can proceed, there is a great need for research that attempts to develop measures of these more abstract but perhaps more theoretically interesting variables.

Most of the propositions in this section contain conflicting findings, so that we must withhold judgment on their validity until further research resolves the differences. However, Proposition 47 is quite firmly supported in drawing a relationship between population size, population change, and foreign conflict. And the studies relevant to Proposition 50 give a good deal of confidence in that relationship as well.

We have already suggested that future research on the societal cluster might well employ the independent variables mentioned above. It is particularly surprising, in light of the attention it has received, that societal modernization has not been correlated with foreign policy patterns. This is one way in which nations really differ. Either as an independent or control variable we believe that modernization is deserving of more attention. Moreover, whatever societal variables are used, our survey shows that more attention should be paid to their impact on the process of foreign policy formation itself.

Chapter X

CULTURAL VARIABLES

Are certain religions more warlike than others? Does the communications system of a state have a crucial impact on foreign policy decision-making? Do nations that speak the same or similar languages have a higher level of interactions than others? What is the connection between ideology and conflict? These are the types of questions that will be considered in this chapter on cultural variables.

PROPOSITION 53: *A nation's ideology exerts an influence on the formulation of foreign policy.*

Three comparative case studies find ideology to be more than rhetoric used to justify a policy. Bandyopadhyaya (1968: 35) reports that in India and Pakistan, "ideology constitutes one of the basic elements of foreign policy." In a content analysis of the speeches of Norwegian, British, and American legislators in the late 1950s, Ruge (1964: 85) finds that the self-image (i.e., ideology) of a nation influences the kind of argument used by legislators in favoring or opposing technical assistance. For example, U.S. debates are carried on in terms of power politics; British debates, in terms of economics and Commonwealth relations; and Norwegian debates, in terms of international peace and understanding.

Ideology seems to be a more potent force in the formulation of policy than is national interest, though scholars have often thought the opposite. The fact that the French-American conflict in the 1960s was seen by leaders in terms of national interest contributed to the containment of the rift between the two; that is, each recognized the security problems of the other and did not challenge the other on this basis. In contrast, the fact that the Soviet-Chinese conflict in the 1960s was seen in terms of ideology contributed to the widening of the schism between the two, for neither recognized the legitimacy of the other's ideology (Brezezinski and Huntington, 1963: 404).

While ideology may be an important determinant in the process of formulating general policy, it is less relevant to making decisions on specific actions. In the three Formosa Straits crises, Sigal (1970: 154) found only a tenuous relationship between the early strategic thought of Mao Tse-tung and Chinese actions toward the United States and Taiwan; he concludes that ideology is meant to be political, not military, even when it concerns such things as war and defense.

Wright would agree with this last paragraph; although he does not specifically compare the influence of ideology and national interest, he does look at the effect of national interest on specific foreign policy acts. His research (1965: 441-442) on 45 conflicts in the twentieth century reveals that the more important are national interests perceived by participants to be involved in a given situation, the greater is the chance of the conflict escalating.

PROPOSITION 54:   *The greater the cultural similarity of two nations, the lower the level of violent behavior between them.*

Rummel (1969: 239) reports that three measures of cultural similarity are positively related to peace between states: they are racial distance, mail A →B/A's domestic mail, and translations A→B/A's total translations. The greater the similarity, the lower the conflict between the two states. The opposite is also true: there is a tendency for states to undertake war against targets which are culturally dissimilar and are regarded as untrustworthy (Haas, 1969a: 86), and to be hostile to dissimilar states (Finlay, Holsti, and Fagen, 1967: 236-237). However, for nations already in violent conflict, cultural and racial similarity will not reduce (or increase) the *intensity* of the violence. The latter finding is also Rummel's (1967a: 187), from research on 779 dyads in 211 violent conflicts between 1820 and 1952.

Richardson presents two findings on cultural variables, one of which modifies, and the other negates, Proposition 54. In his work on over 300 deadly quarrels between 1820 and 1945, he makes this statement (1960: xii): "Similarity of religion seems not to have made for peace, except in the case of Confucianism, but differences of religion have apparently caused war, especially the differences of Christianity and Islam." While this finding only modifies the proposition, the next one pretty much disconfirms it (1960: xi): "Similarity and difference of language seem to have had little influence on the occurrence of wars during this period . . . except that the Chinese language has been correlated with peacefulness and Spanish with warlikeness."

Obviously, then, we must separate the numerous cultural variables into different propositions.

PROPOSITION 55: *The higher the level of nationalist sentiment, the greater the likelihood that a nation will be involved in war.*

Wright considers nationalism an important variable in his research on war. He shows (1964: 212) that the desire of a nationality for self-determination and the desire to incorporate an *irredentum* have both been factors in the frequency of war. According to Wright, nationalistic ideology has several characteristics that lead to war. The people seek "security from attack, stability of their economic life, and development of a distinctive character by economic isolation and self-sufficiency" (1964: 213). The nation also tends "to acquire an attitude of superiority to some or all other peoples, to seek to extend its cultural characteristics throughout the world, and to ignore the claims of other states and of the world community" (1964: 213). But, surprisingly, it is not the intensity or homogeneity of these feelings that is crucial:

The warlikeness of a state is probably more influenced by the methods used to build nationalism and by the rate at which nationalism is intensifying than by the intensity or homogeneity of nationalism actually achieved [Wright, 1964: 220].

Finally, the balance-of-power system is particularly sensitive to nationalism: "either too much or too little nationalism in important states disturbs the equilibrium and causes international tensions" (1964: 219).

PROPOSITION 56: *Dimensions of the national culture are related to a nation's involvement in foreign conflict.*

This important hypothesis has been tested by several scholars using different types of cultural variables. Their findings are lumped together here because there has not been sufficient replication to warrant separate propositions for each of the independent variables; the scope of the existing studies, however, is an encouraging beginning.

The Feierabends operationalize this variable in terms of the level of need achievement. They find (1969: 150-151) that the level of need achievement in 1925 is negatively related to foreign conflict for "high modern" nations, and the level of need achievement in 1950 is positively related for "mid-modern" and "low modern" nations.

Several of the cultural dimensions identified by Cattell (1949: 459-465) exert an influence on foreign conflict behavior. The interested reader should refer to Cattell's study for descriptions of these dimensions. The factor of "conservative patriarchal solidarity versus ferment of release" is positively related to the percentage of the population maintained in military forces (loading = .56). The factor of "cultural pressure versus direct ergic expression" is positively related to the frequency of a nation's participation in wars (loading = .62) and to the number of political clashes with other countries (loading = .63). Finally, the factor of "residual or peaceful progressiveness" is negatively related to government expenditure on armaments, though Cattell notes that there is doubt as to the validity of the measurement of expenditures (loading = .70).

The tendency of a people to desire revenge is another aspect of a nation's culture. In his research on over 300 deadly quarrels from 1820 to 1945, Richardson (1960: xi) includes this statement: "Desire for revenge seems to have been an important cause of war during this period, declining as the inciting war recedes in history but rising slightly after a generation." But ironically, a peace movement can also lead to war:

Peace propaganda has frequently in times of crisis urged particular groups to isolate themselves from areas of contention in order to avoid war and has thereby disintegrated the national community and assured the initiation and subsequent spread of war [Wright, 1964: 266].

As happens so often throughout this book, we can count on Rummel (1968: 204-213) to offer a disconfirmation of the proposition at hand. In his study on 77 nations for the period 1955-1957, he finds little relationship between the psychological motivations of the people and foreign conflict behavior and between national values and foreign conflict behavior.

PROPOSITION 57: *There is a relationship between a nation's religious composition and its voting in the United Nations.*

Rummel's research (1969: 234, 238) finds that Catholic culture is one of five factors which account for most of a nation's voting in the U.N.; and the more similar two nations are in Catholic culture, the more aligned their U.N. voting will be. This correlation between religious similarity and voting alignment will be much weaker for nations at peace than for nations in conflict (Rummel, 1969: 239). Of course, in this research "Catholic culture" may just be another name for Latin America.

With respect to specific votes, there are only two studies using religious variables. Alker (1964: 654-655) finds that religious variables are related to U.N. voting on the "Moslem factor" dimension of voting. And Vincent (1971: 486-490) finds that the factor of "religious homogeneity" accounts for five percent of the variance in the "U.N. intervention" dimension.

PROPOSITION 58:   *The greater the cultural similarity of two nations, the greater is the level of transactions between them.*

Cobb and Elder's study (1970: 135) of 1,176 dyads finds a relationship, although a moderate one, between the cultural homogeneity of two nations and their mutual relevance. Rummel (1969: 239) uses more limited indicators for each variable and finds, for nations in conflict with each other, a high correlation between language similarity and study migrations, tourists, and treaties. He also finds (1969: 238) a correlation between translations of each other's literature and tourist movements, but more so for nations in overt conflict. Deutsch's study (1960b: 48) of 106 nations and 15 North Atlantic nations, though not a dyadic analysis, finds that language and culture are highly correlated with deviations from an indifference model in trade. Finally, Cattell's research (1949: 459) produces a positive relationship between the factor of "cultural pressure vs. direct ergic expression" and the frequency of all types of treaties entered into (loading = .60).

Miscellaneous Findings

For all the importance that has been ascribed to information flows and communications systems in the decision-making literature, there is only one empirical study connecting this variable to foreign policy formation. McGowan's study (1970: 208) of 45 nations reports that "the more mass-media oriented the societal communications system, the more pronounced the degree of political recruitment by rational-legal procedures."

A study by Dowty (1971: 432) is particularly interesting, for two reasons. First, his dependent variable of the existence of "foreign-linked factionalism" is highly relevant in these days of subversion and penetration of national societies. "Foreign-linked factionalism" is defined on page 431 of the study as "the presence within a state of a competing faction that seeks or accepts aid from other states in order to seize or wield power by non-legitimized means." Second, his data on 237 dyadic conflicts is an excellent example of historical research in political science. He takes his data from historical literature covering four periods: the Classical World (280-150 B.C.), India (1347-1526), Europe (1492-1559), and Latin America (1810-1914). His finding relevant to this chapter is that interstate cultural heterogeneity is not related to foreign-linked factionalism, except in the Classical World, which had conditions of extreme heterogeneity.

Evaluation

We cannot yet make a judgment on the validity of the propositions in this section because the amount of research is small. Thus, our suggestion is that more work be done using cultural variables. We are heartened that many different independent cultural variables have been examined: religion, race, language, communications system, nationalism, and ideology. The studies have also been quite broad in scope and diversified in the dependent variables considered.

Political culture is a prominent concept in comparative politics, yet we have found no comparative studies of foreign policy which use this concept as an independent variable predicting foreign policy behavior and the process of policy formation. Yet, variations along the parochial-subject-participant continuum seem highly relevant to the impact of the society at large on foreign policy.[1]

NOTE

1. These concepts are presented in Gabriel A. Almond and Sidney Verba, *The Civic Culture* (Boston: Little, Brown, 1965).

Chapter XI

LINKAGE VARIABLES

Often a foreign policy-maker justifies a particular decision on the basis that the government must honor commitments made in the past to another country. Or he will argue that a particular decision must be taken because the country is obligated by an international treaty. Clearly, the history of a nation's international activity is an important factor in its foreign policy. This variable cluster includes the linkages with other nations made in the past through treaties, trade, membership in international organizations, personal contacts, colonialism, and so forth.

PROPOSITION 59: *Whether or not another nation is a member of the decision-maker's bloc affects how the latter will perceive, and act towards, that nation.*

Zinnes' study (1966: 486) of the pre-World War I crisis finds that nations outside a bloc are seen as more threatening and more unfriendly than nations within the bloc. Taking a somewhat different approach, Siverson (1970: 165) finds that during crisis periods, Israeli and Egyptian decision-makers tend to perceive allies as targets of injury, though at a lower level than their own nation, and see enemies as operating in a favorable environment as the targets of positive acts. These perceptions affect the flow of hostility: there is more hostility transmitted between blocs than within blocs (Zinnes, 1966: 486). However, they do not affect interactions; the frequency of interaction within the bloc is no greater than that between the blocs (Zinnes, 1966: 490).

PROPOSITION 60: *Private and governmental contact between nations does not reduce the chances of their coming into conflict with each other.*

Rummel (1968: 204-13) examines 77 nations for the period 1955-1957 and finds little relationship between the level of international communications or transactions and foreign conflict behavior. Then in another study (1969: 238) he looks at dyads and again finds no relationship between foreign conflict and slightly different independent variables—emigration, communications, and co-memberships in international organizations. Wright (1964: 170) goes even further than Rummel: not only do linkages in the form of economic and cultural contact not reduce the chances of conflict, but the first effect of increasing such contact is to *increase* at a later time the chances of war. Russett (1967: 198) agrees with Wright in his work on conflict between 1946 and 1965: "countries belonging to the same groupings by organizational membership, proximity, or trade are more than twice as likely to fight than are nations which belong to different groups, or to none." Even is these three ties are between nations that are similar in sociocultural characteristics and in U.N. voting behavior, the likelihood of war is still not reduced (Russett, 1967: 199).

The Feierabends report a finding that modifies the proposition. Analyzing different types of nations in their sample of 84 nations for 1955-1961, they find (1969:

150-151) that mail flows are inversely related to foreign conflict for "high modern" nations. And case studies of Brzezinski and Huntington (1963: 404-406) disconfirm the proposition: they conclude that the extent of informal communication, shared experiences, and nongovernmental interaction since World War II contributed to the containment of the French-American rift and the widening of the Soviet-Chinese rift.

Although his dependent variable is defense expenditures and not foreign conflict, Smoker's (1964b: 71-72) longitudinal analysis of Sino-Indian relations between 1950 and 1964 is relevant to this proposition. His conclusion contradicts the proposition and agrees with the Feierabends and Brzezinski and Huntington: there is an inverse relationship between the trade and the total yearly letter rate between China and India and the defense expenditures of India.

PROPOSITION 61: *Treaties between nations have the effect of lessening their foreign conflict behavior toward each other.*

Rummel (1968: 204-213) shows that treaties are the only type of cooperative behavior that may be related to foreign conflict: his finding is not conclusive, nor does he specify the direction of the relationship. Weede (1970: 230) is more definite in a study that analyzes more specific variables for 59 nations from 1955 to 1960: "Nations that have signed many military treaties tend to be involved in less verbal foreign conflict, provided that power is equal." And Brzezinski and Huntington (1963: 406) support him, finding that the extent of formal and informal institutions binding two countries was a factor in containing the friction between the United States and France and in exacerbating the relations between China and the Soviet Union. Wright (1964: 146), although his dependent variable is somewhat different, also confirms the proposition: political arrangements are a major factor influencing the success of disarmament (i.e., decreased conflict).

Wright (1964: 132, 137, 159) presents three other findings that are somewhat different from Proposition 61 but can best be grouped under it. First, he states that ad hoc alliances, as opposed to permanent alliances or confederations, have been most favorable to preserving the balance of power. Second, he makes this statement:

The difficulties which federations, especially those formed by the union of sovereign states, have sometimes encountered in concluding and carrying out international engagements have caused diplomatic friction but have had little direct importance in causing war.

Third, he finds that the legal institution of neutrality (i.e., the absence of treaty ties) has not had much effect in keeping the European powers out of war, but it has enabled smaller states to avoid the wars of the big powers.

PROPOSITION 62: *There is a relationship between the pattern of a nation's linkages and its voting in the U.N.*

First we will deal with the general voting alignment of states and then with their positions on the specific dimensions of U.N. voting. Ellis and Salzberg (1965: 31-32) analyze 100 votes of 24 African nations in the 1960-1961 session and find that the degree of voting alignment of an African nation with other African nations is related to the ratio of exports to the United States, United Kingdom, and France to total exports. Lidstrom and Wiklund (1967: 185) analyze the votes of the Nordic nations in 362 roll calls (1956-1965) and find that treaties with other nations affect voting alignment: Finland—with a treaty of accommodation with the U.S.S.R.—votes more often than other Nordic states with the U.S.S.R., the three NATO countries vote more often with the United States, and Sweden is more often neutral.

Two more general works support the findings of these regional studies. Gareau's (1970: 943) diachronic analysis of U.N. members in "Cold War voting" reports that voting alignment follows the alliance structure of the world for the periods 1947-1955, 1956-1959, 1960-1962, and less well for 1963-1967. Alker and Russett's study (1965: 260) of U.N.

members in four separate years reports that "countries which trade heavily with their regional groups are more likely to vote with the group."

Before moving to the specific dimensions of U.N. voting, we must report a study by Kay (1969: 44) that is related to this proposition. He reports that external ties have affected the general orientation of U.N. activity. Specifically, he finds that the African states, banding together on the basis of their colonial heritage, have made colonialism the chief concern of the U.N. and have pressured the U.N. to issue condemnations of specific actions and requests for sanctions rather than general pronouncements on moral and legal rights.

Alker's study (1964: 654-655) of 70 roll-call votes in the sixteenth session of the General Assembly reports that trade and aid ties are related to U.N. voting on the "East versus West," "North versus South," "Cold War membership," and "U.N. supranationalism" dimensions. The work that he did with Russett (1965: 225-242) confirmed this finding for four different sessions but added one dimension—"Palestine-related" issues. Alker also finds (1964: 654-655) that colonial history is related to U.N. voting on the "East versus West," "North versus South," and "self-determination" dimensions. Again his finding was supported by the study with Russett (1965: 225-242), and again they added one dimension—"supranationalism" issues.

Being more specific in his independent variable, Alker (1964: 654-655) reports a correlation between military alliance with the United States and voting on the "East versus West" dimension. Alker and Russett (1965: 225-242) show that military alliances with the United States and the U.S.S.R. are related to the "East versus West," "North versus South," "Palestine-related," and "Cold War" dimensions. Finally, Vincent (1971: 486, 490), in a cross-sectional analysis of the 1960s that employs the data of Russett (1966) and Alker and Russett (1965), finds that the factor of "U.S. relations" accounts for 19 percent and 4 percent of the variance in the "Eastern voting" and "Iberia" dimensions, respectively.

Political alignment is also related to voting on specific sets of issues, as well as on these broader dimensions of voting. With regard to voting on the international legal activities of the U.N., Western-aligned states favor the status quo; Communist-aligned states oppose the status quo; and non-aligned states are divided, though they lean against the status quo (Todd, 1971: 307-308).

PROPOSITION 63: *There is a positive relationship between a nation's allignment with the West and its support of, and election success in, the United Nations.*

For this proposition we have only two studies, one for each dependent variable. The study of 101 United Nations members in 1963 by Clark, O'Leary, and Wittkopf (1971: 20-21), finds two significant positive correlations of external ties to U.N. support: between military alignment with the West and the "economic" factor of support for all nations, and between agreement with the United States on U.N. roll-call votes and the "economic" factor of support for all nations and the "system-change" factor for less developed and developed nations. The Singer-Sensenig article (1963: 902) on U.N. members between 1946 and 1962 shows that a high degree of alignment with the United States in voting on Cold War issues is related to success in U.N. elections.

PROPOSITION 64: *Previous governmental collaboration is positively associated with transactions at a later period.*

Cobb and Elder's work (1970: 135) on 210 dyads in the North Atlantic area (1952-1964) and 1,176 dyads in the global system (1955) includes two findings that support this proposition. One is that previous collaboration, especially on treaties concerning travel and tourism, promotes "mutual relevance" in both the regional and global system. The other is that wartime alignments in the North Atlantic system predicted to future interchange, particularly mail and tourism. Deutsch (1960b: 48), in a diachronic study of 15 North Atlantic nations and 106 nations in the global system, finds that financial and political association correlate with high deviations from an indifference model in international trade. Alger and Brams (1967: 660) support Deutsch in a study of 119 nations for 1963-1964, finding a moderately strong relationship between number of memberships and shared memberships in IGOs and trade.

Two studies turn around the variables in Proposition 64 and also find a positive relationship. Cobb and Elder (1970: 135) show that in both the regional and the global system, the higher the level of transactions, the higher will be the level of governmental collaboration. And Russett (1967: 207) concludes:

Similar orientations in world politics lead to the growth of trade between countries, and the trade, along with the similar political outlooks, leads on to the growth of international organizations which bind the nations together in a formal manner.

PROPOSITION 65:   *Colonial ties strongly affect the trade and other transactions between nations.*

Brams' dyadic analysis (1966: 889) of over 100 nations reveals that colonial heritage is one of the two most dominating influences in structuring the transaction flow subgroups for trade. Deutsch's diachronic study (1961: 459), though he deals with nations and not dyads, supports Brams: "Colonial empires and spheres of influence, present and to a lesser extent past," are associated with deviations from an indifference model in trade.

If we look at colonial ties in three different stages, the proposition still holds. First there are countries which are still colonies:

For a "normalized" country of 10 million population and a per capita income below $225, colonial status is associated with a strikingly high foreign trade ratio of about 52 percent, as against a ratio of only 37 per cent for soverign countries of the same size and income levels [Deutsch, Bliss, and Eckstein, 1962: 364].

Second, there are countries in the process of decolonization:

Territories recently soverign, and colonial territories near the point of independence . . . showed in 1954 markedly less trade distortion in favor of their present or former "mother countries" than did most of the other colonies" [Deutsch, 1960b: 48] .

Finally, there are countries which were colonies: "Most former colonies continue to trade almost as much with former colonial rulers, and fellow colonies, as they did before independence" (Russett, 1967: 156).

The proposition also holds when transactions other than trade are used as the dependent variable. Brams (1966: 889) reports that colonial heritage is strongly related to the transaction flow subgroups for diplomatic exchanges and shared IGO memberships. Wittkopf (1971: 102), in a study of foreign aid flows between 1961 and 1967, finds a relationship between colonial ties and the aid distributed by France and Britain.

PROPOSITION 66: *There is a positive relationship between linkages in international organizations and diplomatic contact.*

Alger and Brams' study (1967: 660) reports a moderately strong relationship between number of memberships and shared memberships in IGOs and diplomatic exchanges. Russett and Lamb (1969: 49), studying 104 nations for 1963 and 1964, report the same relationship, and also correlate diplomatic exchange to trading groups.

Several studies report the finding that international organizations are by far the most common method of diplomatic contact for most nations—much more so than traditional bilateral exchanges. Hovet's study (1963: 215) of African nations in the United Nations between 1946 and 1962 comes to this conclusion. So do the broader studies by O'Leary (1969: 34) and Alger and Brams (1967: 659-662), both of which examine over 100 nations and international organizations other than the U.N.

PROPOSITION 67: *The existence of an alliance increases the possibility of a nation supporting its ally (and becoming involved in conflict) according to the terms of the pact between them.*

Are alliances mere political paperwork, or do they entail meaningful commitments? In their study of 112 formal alliances involving 82 nations between 1815 and 1914, Singer and Small (1966: 18-19) find that formal alliance commitments increase a nation's propensity to support an ally militarily; also, nations in defense pacts are more likely to come to the defense of their allies than are nations with commitments to remain neutral or merely consult. The result, of course, is that the chances of an allied nation staying out of war were not good during the period studied (Singer and Small, 1969: 526-527). This relationship weakened, however, when Singer and Small (1969: 527, 539, 542) controlled for duration of membership in the system, and they admit that they have no plausible theoretical explanation for this finding. Another result of the historical flow of alliances has been the fluctuations in the balance of power (Wright, 1964: 130).

The findings of Singer and Small are supported by a more limited study done by Choucri and North (1969: 49, 56). They examine the activities of the members of the Triple Entente and Dual Alliance for the period 1870-1914 and report that the most pronounced paths to violence are from alliance commitments.

Russett (1963: 109) studies a special situation of coming to the aid of an allied nation. The focus of his analysis is seventeen cases from 1935 to 1961 in which a defending power had expressed some kind of commitment to protect a threatened "pawn" from impending attack. He finds that ties in the form of military cooperation, political interdependence, and economic interdependence led to successful deterrence of the threatening nation.

What happens to relations between alliance partners in the years after the pact expires? Two studies are relevant to this question. Richardson (1960: xi) makes this statement: "Allies in one war may become enemies in the next, but alliances seem to have had some influence in preventing war between former allies. That influence, however, declines with the passage of time since the war alliance." Singer and Small (1966: 18) find that in the three years after the expiration of an alliance, the propensity to fight for and fight against the former ally goes up, while the propensity to remain neutral decreases.

PROPOSITION 68: *There is a relationship between the bloc ties and colonial ties of a nation and its interaction patterns in the international system.*

Brams' analysis of 121 nations in 1964 and 1965 operationalizes interaction as diplomatic visits between nations, which he calls a measure of influence. He finds (1969: 599) that nations influenced by both superpowers tend to be nonaligned nations, nations aligned with one bloc but favoring closer ties with the other bloc, or nations which are centers of conflict between the two blocs of their proxies. Also, Brams finds (1969: 599) that the most "influential" and least "influential" states tend to be small nations with asymmetrical ties principally to major powers in large mutual influence sets.

McGowan correlates ties through colonialism with interaction. His study (1969: 217-218) of 30 African states for 1963 and 1964 finds that those states which follow an inactive-dependent pattern of interaction are former French colonies; those that follow a transitional pattern are of mixed colonial heritage, and those that follow an active-independent pattern are North African-Arab states.

The usual distinction for political alignment is Western, Communist, and nonaligned. In an unusual departure from this type of study, Keim (1971: 290-291) divides the latter group into two: nonaligned nations are those that adopt a specific policy of nonalignment, and unaligned nations are those that have made less positive decisions to remain

uncommitted, i.e., they have no active policy of nonalignment. Keim's dependent variable is uniqueness of conflict
patterns. He finds that at higher levels of power, nonaligned
nations show more uniqueness in conflict patterns than do
unaligned nations, but the distinction does not hold at lower
levels of power.

Miscellaneous Findings

Alker and Puchala (1968: 316) have done a study of a
particular set of external ties and their effect on the
economic growth of nations. Examining the members of the
European Common Market in a diachronic analysis of the
period 1928-1963, they find that membership in the organization has increased each nation's share of world trade, has
made each more independent economically, and has produced a rate of economic growth higher than that of the
United States or the members of the European Free Trade
Association.

Wallensteen (1968: 262) does a comparative case study of
ten instances of economic sanctions between 1933 and 1967,
focusing on the relationship of trade ties to the sending of
sanctions. His findings are that trade with the receiver has
been of low importance for most senders, and that trade with
the sender has been of high importance for most receivers. He
also reports that the actual reduction in trade has been less
than planned by the sender, and that after a two year period,
trade has returned to previous levels.

McGowan's research (1969: 217-218) on thirty African
nations for 1963-1964 uses the variable of linkages to study
the general foreign policy behavior of these nations. He finds
that the foreign policy options of the African states are
interrelated in the following way: decolonization is dependent indirectly on interaction with the Communist world and
directly on diplomatic participation in the international
political system.

Hoadley and Hasegawa (1971: 153-154) study linkages to

determine what are the factors that make linkages effective—
with "effectiveness" defined in terms of achieving the goals
of the individuals and groups concerned. Their research
focuses on the political, ideological, economic and quasi-
diplomatic linkages between China and Japan from 1950 to
1970. Their findings are that "material linkages tend to be
more effective than immaterial linkages," and that "linkages
with internally secure link-points tend to be more effective
than linkages with internally insecure link-points."

Finally, we can report a study which deals with the
absence of previous external ties. Neuchterlein (1969: 622),
examining the alliances of Iceland, Thailand, and Australia
with the United States, shows that "the absence of a colonial
tradition enhances a small state's willingness to accept an
alliance with a great power."

Evaluation

We have a good start in research that tries to account for
foreign policy output in terms of a nation's past linkages.
Both variables have been operationalized in many different
ways, so that our propositions cover a wide range of linkages
and all the major kinds of foreign policy behavior. There is an
excellent foundation; future research should validate the
components of that foundation and then build upon it. In
particular, it might concentrate on the weaknesses apparent
in this section: resolution of the contradictory findings in
Proposition 60, separation and further support of the
independent variables in Proposition 62 and 68, examination
of alignment with others besides the Western nations in
Proposition 63, and testing Proposition 59 with other cases.

These propositions give strong support to the idea that ties
to other nations are a major influence on foreign policy. In
Chapter XV, we will see how these ties feed back onto the
internal environment and become a major influence in
domestic politics. But these two topics do not exhaust the
possibilities of research on linkage politics.[1] One would

like to know the relative potencies of the various kinds of ties; for example, whether colonial ties are more important than trade ties or diplomatic ties, and whether the issue-area affects these relative potencies. And one would like to be able to identify those "linkage groups" which are directly concerned with the various ties and study their role as a specific actor in the foreign policy-making process.

A final way in which the concept of linkages can be fruitfully employed in comparative foreign policy studies is diachronically. Clearly, the basic idea is to treat linkages at time t as predictors to behavior at t + 1. Empirical work in the area of foreign policy has been excessively cross-sectional—examining variables at only one point in time. The concept of linkage variables requires us to introduce time lags into our research which can only serve to strengthen its analytical and explanatory power.

NOTE

1. See James N. Rosenau (ed.) *Linkage Politics* (New York: Free Press, 1969); most of the papers collected in this volume are theoretical; a few are empirical.

Chapter XII

OTHER NATIONS' POLICIES

Until this point we have been concerned with the effect of characteristics of the national society upon its foreign policy behavior. In this section we change our focus to examine the effect of the foreign policy behavior of one society on another. The actions of international actors directed at the nation under analysis impinge upon both the internal characteristics and the foreign policy behavior of the latter. To the extent that others' policies influence a nation, we can say that the receiving nation is *penetrated* by other actors.[1]

PROPOSITION 69: *The support of other nations is an important factor in various kinds of international activity.*
    The dependent variable in this proposition can be no more specific because the findings related to it are diverse in their objects of study. It has been found that violent conflict activity requires the support of other nations. The failure of

Somalia and Morocco to win support for their respective positions helped to contain the border disputes in which they were involved (Touval, 1966: 646). In the Middle East, between 1953 and 1965, the support of other nations in terms of arms was crucial to escalation:

if the 1950 Tripartite arms rationing scheme had not broken down following the initial Soviet-Egyptian arms deal in 1955, defense spending as a percent of GNP in the two major countries, Egypt and Israel, would have remained stable although at a comparatively high level" [Lambelet, 1971: 166].

In fact, wars have on occasion been prevented if there are actors not only denying their support to each side, but also actively exerting a pacifying influence (Richardson, 1952: 219).

The absence of support also has an effect on the success of economic sanctions: these are more likely to work if the target nation appears to be isolated in the international system (Wallensteen, 1968: 262). If a very small nation is isolated, that is, if it does not have the support of the industrial regions, then it may not even be able to maintain its membership as a sovereign state in the international system (Vellut, 1967: 266).

Wolfers' analysis of Britain and France between the two world wars contains this finding (1940: 381): because the two nations did not support each other on their estimates of the German threat, their activities worked at cross-purposes—France trying to organize preponderant force, and Britain trying to achieve a better balance of power through conciliation. Fox looks at five neutral states in World War II in terms of the play of demands and supports and reports (1959: 187):

Instead of moving to the side of the less powerful and thereby helping to restore the balance, they tended to comply with the demands of the more powerful and thus to accentuate any shifts in the balance of forces caused by changing fortunes of war or prospects of ultimate victory.

Finally, Nuchterlein examines the relationship of support to alliance durability. He finds (1969: 622), on the basis of a study of U.S. alliances with Iceland, Thailand, and Australia, that alliance durability depends on agreement of the partners on the nature and source of the principal security threat and on the continued willingness of the protector power to use its strength to deter and/or defeat the common enemy.

PROPOSITION 70: *There is a relationship between the foreign policy acts that a nation directs at another and the responding acts of the target nation.*

Several studies of different situations, some more general and some specific, confirm this proposition. The broadest study is Dehio's research on four European state systems between 1494 and 1945. He finds (1963: 3-15) that if a nation acts, others react: specifically, his conclusion is that the dynamics of the international state system are the result of the attempts of nations to gain supremacy and the subsequent attempts of coalitions to stop challenging powers. Next in scope is the Feierabends' work (1969: 146) on 84 nations in a six-year period, which finds that "external aggression expressed is highly related to amount of aggression received." Then there is the research of Phillips (1971: 31, 44-45), similar to the work of the Feierabends in that it concentrates on only the conflictual side of foreign policy activity. Phillips does a cross-sectional and longitudinal analysis of 65 nations for the year 1963, using 23 indicators of foreign conflict behavior from the DON data. He finds a direct relationship between conflict sent and conflict received, but the relationship is far from being 1: 1; at least sixty percent of the variance in conflict sent is independent of that received. Responses from the environment are in kind—e.g., diplomatic conflict sent is met with a diplomatic response. In addition, the variation in conflict sent and received by nations is highly structured, centering around five patterns that are constant for longitudinal as well as cross-sectional analysis: negative communications, official military violence, unofficial violence, warning and defensive acts (sabre rattling), and negative sanctions.

Less broad in scope is Gamson and Modigliani's work (1965: 61-62) on interactions between the Soviet Union and (unspecified) Western nations for the period 1946-1953. They find that in periods of confrontation, Western refractory behavior is associated with Soviet conciliatory behavior; in periods of nonconfrontation, Western conciliatory behavior is associated with Soviet conciliatory behavior. Also, radical and violent shifts in Western behavior, rather than a steady policy with moderate adjustments, lead to Soviet concilatory behavior. These conclusions are generally confirmed by Etzioni's work (1968: 428) on the United States and the Soviet Union, for a six-month period in 1963. He reports that the unilateral gestures made by the United States were at first suspected, but eventually were accepted and then reciprocated. This pattern of reciprocal unilateral moves eased tensions during the period, and if the moves were transformed into multilateral measures, tensions were further reduced. Conversely, when the flow of actions stopped, tension reduction stopped also.

Several studies of very specific interactions—in alliances, in bargaining, and in crises—confirm these more general findings. Brzezinski and Huntington's work on two alliances (1963: 405-406) shows that unilateral moves are associated with hostile acts: if one member of an alliance moves unilaterally, the other will express hostility, and the result is a widened schism between the two nations. Jensen's longitudinal analysis (1963: 528) of Soviet and American disarmament negotiations between 1946 and 1960 finds that the concessions of one nation are related to the reciprocating concessions of the other nation in the same round or the next round. If a nation's consessions are not reciprocated, it will reduce its level of concessions in the next round. In an analysis of the Cuban missile crisis of 1962, Holsti, Brody and North (1969: 687) report that "as the level of violence in the actions of one party increased or decreased, the actions of the other party tended to follow a similar pattern." This type of reciprocity is also evident in the Middle East crises, where in the period 1953-1965, the arms race was a pattern of reactions and responses that, in the absence of disturbances, fairly rapidly (4-5 years) attained a static equilibrium value or an equilibrium growth rate (Lambelet, 1971: 166).

PROPOSITION 71: *The pattern of threats nations direct at each other and the subsequent level of fear affects the foreign policies of nations.*

Smoker has examined the relationship of fear and arms escalation. In studies (1963: 72; 1964a: 62) of the United States and Soviet Union between 1948 and 1960, he finds that the introduction of nuclear weapons led to the emergence of a fear factor or "submissiveness effect" which causes cyclical arms races. When the weight of fear becomes too great, the arms escalation slows down; this cools off the international climate, the submissiveness effect switches off, and nations return to escalation.

Siverson's study of the 1956-1957 Suez crisis can be interpreted as another test of the fear factor, though he himself does not make the connection. His content analysis (1970: 164) of the statements of Egyptian and Israeli decision-makers reveals that "perceptions of injury were still relatively high even as violence was *decreasing.*" We can theorize that the fear factor remained in effect, causing continued perceptions of injury, even as the actual violence was decreasing.

Schwartz (1967: 486, 488) finds that threats have had two effects on foreign policy in eight crises between the United States and the U.S.S.R. in the period 1950 to 1964. The higher the level of threats, the greater is the receptivity of decision-makers to messages from opponents. And the more direct the crisis confrontation, and thus the greater the threat, the more credible does escalation become.

The management of threats and fear can be an important determinant of the success of foreign policy. In their study of

Laos, Cuba and Vietnam, George et al. (1971: 216) find that the opponent's fear of unacceptable levels of military escalation is one of the eight conditions favoring the success of United States coercive diplomacy; of these eight conditions, this is one of the three most important.

External threat can affect a policy of international unification. Haas (1968: xxxiii), in his analysis of the European Coal and Steel Community, makes this statement: "A helpful but by no means indispensable, condition [for international unification] is the existence of an external threat, real or imagined."

PROPOSITION 72: *The amount of foreign aid received is related to a nation's activity in the United Nations.*

Ellis and Salzberg (1965: 31), in their analysis of 100 votes of 24 African members during the 1960-1961 session, report that degree of voting alignment with other African nations is related to foreign aid per capita received from the United States and Britain. But Wittkopf partially contradicts them, although he focuses on voting position and not voting alignment. For the period 1961-1967, he finds (1971: 136-137) no relationship between U.N. voting and aid received from the DAC nations, with the exception of U.S. aid received.

Singer and Sensenig study the activities of member nations in U.N. elections between 1946 and 1962; their n varies between 53 and 105. The conclusion (1963: 602) they reach is that a high level of economic and military aid received from the United States is positively related to success in U.N. elections.

Clark, O'Leary, and Wittkopf correlate aid received to support of the U.N. For the 101 members in their study, they find (1971: 20-21) two significant positive correlations: between foreign aid received from the West and the "system-conforming" and "economic" factors of support for all nations and for the less developed nations, and between multilateral aid received and the "system-conforming" and "economic" factors of support for less developed nations.

PROPOSITION 73: *The nature of a diplomatic protest and the method of delivering it affect the success of the protest.*

There is only one, very limited work relevant to this proposition, and that is McKenna's analysis (1962: 195-200) of five American diplomatic protests. First, he finds that a protest is more likely to be successful when it is based on the prospect of strained relations rather than on the abstract persuasive force of argument. A second finding is that "in the successful cases, United States' expectations had been firm; the valuation of objectives, on its part, had run from low to moderately high; the valuation of concession, on the part of the recipients, from moderately high to high." Third, he finds that success is dependent on the cost to the target nation of yielding relative to the cost of acquiescence. Finally, he states that it cannot be decided from the case studies whether a severe or a mild attitude in delivering the protest leads to its success, which illustrates the problems inherent in the case study approach—more important variables than cases!

PROPOSITION 74: *The foreign policy acts of one nation affect public opinion and attitudes in another nation.*

Most public opinion surveys are analyses at the individual level only; for example, a study will correlate the individual's social background with his opinions on a particular foreign policy. While public opinion is a factor in foreign policy-making, these studies cannot be included in this survey because neither of the variables concerns "identifiable acts undertaken by the official representatives of the nation." However, there are several works which qualify as comparative studies of foreign policy.

Almond (1968: 92-106) has studied the effect of the Soviet Sputnik on the citizens of Britain, West Germany, France, Italy, and the United States with survey data for the years 1957-1960. His findings support Proposition 74. Each major attainment in the satellite competition produced substantial shifts in estimates of scientific capability, smaller shifts in estimates of military capability, and a sharp drop in the percentage of those who believed the United States would be militarily superior in 20 or 25 years. These changing estimates led to demands to "meet the challange" through economic, military, and educational means, and to a drop in support of the Republican foreign policy leadership in the United States. They also led to shifts in opinions in other areas: decreased support for American policy on mutual troop withdrawals in Europe, increased support for continuing international negotiations on any topic and for a more active role in the U.N. Finally, Sputnik produced opinion shifts in favor of neutrality in all countries except Germany and, in a question of whom one would side with in the event of war, it reinforced the pro-American sentiment in Britain, reinforced neutralist sentiment in France, and produced little change in Germany and Italy, where opinion was already divided.

The donation of foreign aid is an important factor in public opinion, for example, U.S. aid is mentioned in the newspapers of India and Pakistan on an average of once every two and a half to five and a half days (Andreas, 1969: 170). Editors of newspapers defined the aid relationship as a reciprocal one; but when the United States intervened politically or militarily in another recipient nation, then opinion shifted toward seeing the objectives of the two sides of the aid relationship as incompatible (Andreas, 1969: 11-174).

PROPOSITION 75: *The impact of a foreign economic system influences domestic politics and foreign policy-making in the dominated country.*

In a study of eighteen Latin American nations in 1956, Midlarsky and Tanter (1967: 218) confirm this proposition with the finding that the economic presence of the United States in fourteen nondemocratic Latin American nations leads to hostility toward the United States and an increasing level of economic development, both of which then lead to revolution and its accompanying violence. They report that this model holds less well for all eighteen nations studied, and not at all for the four democratic nations. In fact, in the latter, there is a strong *negative* relationship between U.S. economic presence and hostility towards the United States (Midlarsky and Tanter, 1967: 215).

The Midlarsky-Tanter model is supported in a general way by two other studies. Chalmers' comparative case study of Latin America (1969: 88) reports that the presence of foreign economic factors has some negative effect on the level of stability of political institutions. Vellut's comparative case studies of small African nations (1967: 266) finds that the nature and origin of international investments "influences the political orientation and, more generally, the internal structure of those new countries."

Turning now to the influence of a foreign economic system on foreign policy-making, we have only Bunker's comparative diachronic analysis of Peru between 1958 and 1966. He finds (1969: 295-296) that the U.S. economic system exerts a strong influence on the formulation of foreign policy and that international actors other than nation-states have important roles in this influence process. This does not mean that Peru's foreign policy is simply reactive, for Bunker does find cases in which Peru has taken the initiative in influencing others.

PROPOSITION 76:   *The donation of foreign aid gives the donor influence in the internal politics and the foreign policy of the recipient.*

Walters (1970: 245), in his study of Soviet and American foreign aid since World War II, states that "economic assistance has proven to be a useful instrument for establishing political entree, maintaining a presence, and gaining access to decision-makers in less developed countries." The result of this penetration has been that the donor can influence the political orientation of the recipient, as well as the specific development projects underway (Walters, 1970:

239, 245; Tansky, 1967: 176). The United States has wielded more such influence than the Soviet Union because of the activist position it adopts in the administration of its aid programs. But the influence of the donor has been modest at best:

There are no cases where aid has changed the allegiance of a less developed country in the cold war, and there are few cases where even a dominant aid presence has assured a rapport between recipient and donor on major issues of foreign policy [Walters, 1970: 242].

Even very specific attempts at influence—in the form of sanctions withholding aid—have been largely unsuccessful (Wallensteen, 1968: 262). In fact, the donation of aid has sometimes exacerbated relations between donor and recipient. Walters (1970: 234) finds this to have been the case when the United States and the Soviet Union have rescheduled payments to alleviate the debt service burden of recipient nations.

PROPOSITION 77:   *Foreign aid speeds the economic and political development of the recipient nation.*

Assuming that development is the goal of foreign aid, does aid accomplish its purpose? Walters' research (1970: 238, 245) shows that large amounts of Soviet and American aid, especially the latter because of its duration, scope, and diversity, have indeed contributed to economic development. Tansky's work (1967: 166, 174) on Soviet and American aid to Turkey, India, and the U.A.R. supports him on this. Tansky also finds that aid in the form of food is often most effective in alleviating conditions which retard economic development.

Tansky's findings (1967: 176) are modified somewhat when he shows that although American aid has stimulated economic development, the recipients have not been able to dispense with that aid, nor have they become more stable politically because of it. Research by Pincus (1965: 85) supports this modified stance: "economic aid is often a small factor among many variables that determine underdeveloped countries' economic growth and political change."

In research on eighteen Latin American nations, Tanter (1970: 177) examines the relationship between foreign aid and political development. Specifically, he tests the causal model that foreign aid leads to social mobilization, which then leads to civil violence. His data cover the period 1953-1963: four indicators of U.S. penetration are measured for 1953-1961; one indicator each for the intervening variables of urbanization and mobilization are measured for 1960; and the dependent variable of civil violence is from Gurr's (1966) data covering the years 1961-1963. Using partial correlation, Tanter does not find the indirect link that he expected; instead, there is a direct link between American economic assistance per capita and American private economic presence per capita to social mobilization and to magnitude of civil violence. However, there is an indirect link from U.S. *military assistance per capita* to magnitude of civil violence through urbanization and social mobilization. Tanter concludes that "a maximum of about 30 per cent of the total magnitude of civil violence 1961-63 can be explained by one of the types of external financial assistance or economic presence in conjunction with urbanisation and social mobilization."

Using a measure of political development rather than just a measure of civil violence, Wolf (1965: 882, 885; 1967: 103-105, 122) also studies the impact of U.S. aid on Latin America. His research covers twenty nations for the decade of the 1960s. The only significant relationship he finds is between total U.S. economic aid and level of political development (r_s = .47). He finds no relationship between U.S. economic aid per capita and level of political development, and no relationship between either of these variables and change in the level of political development during this period. In addition, there is no significant correlation between amount of military aid received and level of political development or change in the development level.

Miscellaneous Findings

Vital (1971: 125) studies the impact of the policies of large states on smaller ones. In a comparative case study of the Czech-German conflict (1930s), the Israeli-Soviet conflict (1950s-1960s), and the Finnish-Soviet conflict (post-World War II), he concludes that in an effort to maintain or expand its presence in a region, the great power is compelled to prevent its small ally from foundering; the more uncongenial this role becomes, the stronger is the incentive to end the one-sided protectorate and institute full political control.

Hanrieder's diachronic analysis (1967: 234) of West Germany relates other's policies to penetration. He finds that two of the factors facilitating the penetration of West Germany by the international system were the influence of U.S. occupation on institutions and the dependence on external support and regulation for gradual restoration of sovereignty.

Brams' study of influence relationships (1969: 599) finds that the more influential a nation is, the more likely it will be prone to behavior provocative to others. Fox also studies influence relationships in her analysis of five neutral states in World War II. She finds (1959: 180-182) that the influence of small states in the matter of retaining their neutrality depended upon the span of attention which the great power devoted to its demands on the neutral nation.

McGowan correlates foreign aid received with interaction. His study (1968: 290) of 32 African nations between 1963 and 1965 finds that states which receive more foreign aid from all sources are high interactors, while those receiving less aid are low interactors.

Evaluation

The reader has probably noticed that this section includes propositions of two different types. Those propositions that relate other's policies to the foreign policy of the target nation are concerned with the *causes* of the latter's behavior. Those propositions that relate the other's policies to the domestic politics of the target nation are concerned with the *consequences* of the former's behavior. When we consider, then, that there are really two parts to this section, we see that the research employing other's policies is quite limited. In addition, many of the dependent variables used in the propositions are very general; future research must break these down into their components and then derive more specific propositions.

Proposition 70 is an interesting example of research. Studies on very different levels all combine to lend support to the hypothesis. Dehio examines the very broad sweep of international politics. On a middle-range level is the work of the Feierabends, Phillips, Gamson and Modigliani, and Etzioni—all of whom look at broad, but carefully delineated, types of activity. Then there are the analyses of Brzezinski and Huntington, Jensen, Lambelet, and Holsti, Brody, and North; these scholars examine a very specialized type of activity, but they come to the same conclusion as the much broader research on this proposition.

If a nation's domestic politics or foreign policy is affected by the policies of another government, then that nation is a *penetrated society*.[2] All of the propositions in this section show that nations are indeed penetrated, but they do not show the degree of penetration or the dependence of penetration on the types of acts directed at nations. What are the processes by which the traditional national political system becomes a penetrated political system—i.e., a different conceptual unit in which the basic political processes of the soceity are changed? These provacative ideas of Rosenau deserve more empirical investigation.

NOTES

1. James N. Rosenau, "Pre-Theories and Theories of Foreign Policy," pp. 65-71 in R. B. Farrell (ed.) *Approaches to Comparative and International Politics* (Evanston, Ill.: Northwestern University Press, 1966).

2. *Ibid.*

Chapter XIII

SYSTEMIC VARIABLES

The second of the two sets of variables which influence foreign policy from outside the nation-state are characteristics of the international system such as geographic location, degree of integration of a nation into the system, status rank within the system, the characteristics of international organizations, and the level of violent conflict in the system. Many theorists, such as those in the geopolitical school, have considered international system variables the major determinant of foreign policy. Here they are considered as only one of a field of forces determining foreign policy behavior. This is the only assumption that is tenable until research demonstrates the "relative potencies" of all the variable categories in our framework.

PROPOSITION 78: *Variations in the external environment tend to be related to variations in foreign policy over time.*

This proposition states in testable form the relationship postulated in the framework—that systemic variables affect foreign policy. In their research on 82 nations (time period unspecified), East and Gregg (1967: 265) support the hypothesis: "Nations' actions in the international system are systematically rather than randomly associated with their . . . international situation." Furthermore, when East and Gregg break down action into cooperative and conflict types, they find that both of these, but especially conflict, are associated more with variations in international situation than with variations in domestic situation. Wright (1964:156) supports them on this.

When the dependent variable of the proposition is restricted to a particular policy rather than the general foreign policy of a nation, these findings may be reversed. In a study of Germany, Japan, and Italy since World War II, Jensen (1969b: 322) finds that over the years the domestic environment has become a more potent variable in influencing the national security policy process; the regional and contiguous environments have not been major factors, except during periods of internal political instability, when their impact becomes greater.

Cohen, on the other hand, does find that the external environment is an important factor in specific policies. His comparative case study (1969: 139-142) concludes that the international environment has been a socializing influence on American and Soviet leaders, especially in the area of nuclear restraint and the limitations of power. He is supported by a comparative case study done by Holsti and Sullivan (1969: 153). They report that specific international events since World War II have had a socializing influence on Chinese and French leaders in their alliance policy, leading to the movement of both nations away from their alliance partners.

War, of course, is a major systemic determinant of the images of decision-makers that are relevant to the general process of foreign policy formulation. Burgess (1968: 144) has studied the effect of World War II on Norway's leaders.

Elite images were radically changed as a result of the war: it was no longer believed that the rules of international law would be operational in wartime to preserve neutrality, and Norway was seen as "exposed" and "strategic" rather than as peripheral to the interactions of great powers.

PROPOSITION 79:   *Geographic contiguity tends to increase a nation's involvement in foreign conflict.*

Weede's research (1970: 231) using the DON data for 59 nations for the period 1955-1960 shows that "nations contiguous to many other nations are likely to participate in more violent foreign conflict than geographically isolated states." In this finding he is supported by Richardson's and Wright's studies of war. Richardson (1960: x, xiii) concludes that geographic relations affect a nation's war-proneness: "States have tended to become involved in wars in proportion to the number of states with which they have common frontiers." But he modifies this finding with this statement (1960: x-xi):

The actual occurrence of war has been far less than would be expected from the opportunities for war presented by geographical contiguity. Such occurrences have been even less, proportionately, as the opportunities for war have increased through the advance of air and sea power.

Wright (1964: 122, 305) finds that "geographic frontiers marking the transition from one economy to another have often been the scene of war," so that international stability is promoted by a moderate geographic separation of states having differences with each other.

Rummel's research on 164 and 182 dyads in 1955 provides the only disconfirming finding. He finds (1969: 235) little correlation between number of borders with other nations and foreign conflict behavior.

What is the effect on war involvement if a nation's own territories are not all contiguous? Wright (1964: 168-169) finds that strategic vulnerability arising from scattered territories has tended to increase the affected state's involvement in war. Merritt's research, though his dependent variable is not war involvement, can also be cited here. In a comparative case study (1969: 268-269) of Greece in the Golden Age, the Anglo-American community of the eighteenth century, Pakistan, and West Germany-West Berlin, he concludes that territorial noncontiguity makes the state dependent on the external environment for communication among its various parts and more susceptible to the influence and intervention of other states.

PROPOSITION 80:   *There is a positive relationship between international alliance aggregation and the onset of war.*

The Correlates of War Project has created data on the number of alliances in the system and the number of wars between 1816 and 1965. The analysis focuses on a varying number of nations, depending on the time period, and time is treated longitudinally and is lagged. Support for Proposition 80 depends on the time period. In the nineteenth century, the relationship was the opposite of that stated in the proposition: the level of alliance aggregation was negatively related to the onset of war (Singer and Small, 1968: 282; Small and Singer, 1969: 275). Thus, these international arrangements were an effective means of maintaining peace. Not so in the twentieth century. The relationship for this century is positive, and almost as strong as it was for the previous century (Singer and Small, 1968: 282; Small and Singer, 1969: 275). Even when the alliance structure becomes bipolar, the same relationship holds for both centuries (Singer and Small, 1968: 282).

Has the creation of intergovernmental organizations been any more effective in keeping the peace than have alliances? The answer for the whole time period is no: there is no relationship between the creation and continuation of intergovernmental organizations and a reduction in the number and severity of wars (Singer and Wallace, 1970: 538).

PROPOSITION 81: *The greater the amount of status discrepancy in the international system, the greater the level of international violence.*

If a nation's achieved status is different from its ascribed status, we might expect it to engage in foreign conflict behavior as it attempts to balance the two types of status. Achieved status is usually measured in terms of economic and/or military power, and ascribed status is viewed as diplomatic prestige or activity. On this basis, the U.A.R. is clearly an example of a nation in which there is status discrepancy.

In a study focusing on 120 nations for the period 1948-1964, East (1972: 306) finds a moderate relationship between status discrepancy and international violence that increases with one- and two-year time lags. In a broader study, Wallace's (1971: 28-31) findings are somewhat different. For a varying number of nations between 1820 and 1964, he uses an index of achieved status based on five measures of power capability and an index of ascribed status based on the number of diplomatic missions received. There is no relationship between status discrepancy and the magnitude and severity of international war with a lag of zero or five years. With a lag of ten years, a statistically significant relationship is found; and at a lag of fifteen years, the measures of status inconsistency taken together account for 56 per cent and 38 per cent of the two measures of war, respectively. When the 144-year period was divided into three segments, the correlation was still significant at a lag of ten and fifteen years, but it varied with the indicator of power capability. As is often the case, Wallace can offer only ad hoc explanations of why the lags of 10 and 15 years are important, while lags of one or five years are not.

PROPOSITION 82: *The "distance" between states in terms of power and societal attributes is positively related to the instability and violence in the international system.*

Do states that are unlike each other tend to more violence than states which have similar characteristics? The proposition answers affirmatively, but the relevant findings are not all in agreement; the majority of them support the proposition, but several disconfirm it. Future research may be able to explain the discrepancy in terms of the specific type of power or societal variable used.

North and Choucri (1968: 130) look at the distance between nations in nine dyads of opposing members of the Triple Entente and Dual Alliance in terms of five measures of capability: amount of territory, productivity, commercial capability, military strength, and national status. These five factors account for the defense allocations of these states in the 44 years prior to World War I. Wright (1964: 122, 148) concentrates just on military power and supports Proposition 82. But he goes on to state that quantitative equality in arms will not, in itself, assure stability in the system.

Wright (1964: 294) looks at distance between nations in terms of population growth rate. He finds that "differentials of population pressure in neighboring areas, if generally known to the inhabitants of the overpopulated area and if maintained by artificial barriers to trade and migration, tend to international violence." This is especially true if such neighbors are traditional rivals and must provide for their own defense rather than relying on others.

Other societal variables are also relevant. Haas (1968b: 109) looks at demotypes (aggregated human elements) and at attitudes and concludes that if these are distributed unevenly throughout the system, the probability of war is high. Haas' research is limited, however, covering only the period 1955 through 1960.

Two studies contradict these findings. In research that employs path analysis and focuses on the period 1870-1914, Choucri and North (1969: 49) find that the *lesser* the distance between members of the opposing alliances, the higher their respective levels of violence. Singer (1972: 267), in his summary of the Correlates of War Project, states:

most inter-state wars are between nations which are not only close together geographically, but quite similar on most other attribute dimensions—casting some doubt on the old "have/have not" interpretation; for extra-systemic wars, of course, the distances and dissimilarities are considerable.

Finally, Russett (1967: 198) disagrees with both the positive and the negative relationships. In his study of conflict between 1946 and 1965, he finds, using factor analysis, that countries that cluster together in terms of sociocultural similarity and similarity of U.N. voting behavior are neither more nor less likely than other states to fight each other.

PROPOSITION 83: *There is a relationship between a nation's regional position and its voting in the U.N.*

Using the caucus groups delineated by Hovet, Alker (1964: 653) relates membership in a caucus group to voting position on seventy roll calls in the sixteenth General Assembly session. He reports these connections: Old Europeans versus Soviet bloc on "East versus West" issues; Africans, Arabs, and Asians versus Soviet bloc and to a lesser extent Old Europeans on "North versus South" issues; Africans, particularly the Casablanca group, versus Old Europeans on "self-determination" issues; Arab states versus Casablanca group and Africans on "Moslem factor" issues; and Soviet bloc versus Africans and Asians on "U.N. supranationalism" issues. In a different study, Alker (1969: 706-707) examines 52 roll calls between 1947 and 1963 and reaches the conclusion that "*within* the West supranationalism is not an anti-communist reaction, while among non-Western states supranationalism is both an anti-communist and an anti-colonial disposition."

Rather than analyze caucus groups or ill-defined regions such as "West" and "non-West," Alker and Russett (1965: 225-242) derive their regional groupings through a factor analysis of national attributes. For voting in four separate sessions they find that regional grouping is related to voting on the "East versus West" and "North versus South" issues. They also report relationships between "anti-Soviet" grouping and the "supranationalism" dimension of voting, "Arab" grouping and the "Palestine-related" dimension, and "Old European" grouping and the "Palestine-related" and "self-determination" dimensions. Russett (1966: 338; 1967: 77) also uses factor analysis to define regions in two studies, one on voting in 1957-1958 and 1963-1964, and the other on voting in 1963. His conclusion in both studies is the same: on "Cold War" issues, the "Western Community" and the "Brazzaville Africans" oppose the "Afro-Asians" and the "Communists;" on "intervention in Africa" issues the "Western Community" and "Iberia" oppose the "Brazzaville Africans," "Afro-Asians," and "Communists;" on "supranationalism" issues the "Communists" oppose the "Brazzaville Africans" and the "Western Community."

Jacobsen (1967: 146, 156) operationalizes the variable "regional grouping" in yet a fourth way, by looking at the center-periphery dimension, and examines national voting position and dyadic voting agreement. His study covers the five Nordic countries for the years 1946 to 1953. One finding is that voting agreement in the U.N. is highest in central dyads, lower in central-periphery dyads, and lowest in periphery dyads. The other finding is that the center-periphery dimension is a more influential factor than the NATO non-NATO dimension in national voting position, except on East-West issues of high conflict, where the influence of the latter dimension is greater.

PROPOSITION 84: *A state's regional position is related to its support of the U.N.*

Only two studies related regional position to support of the United Nations. Vincent's survey (1968: 928-929) of 68 permanent delegations in 1968 reports that "if a state is close to the U.S.S.R. and China, delegate attitudes will be negative and static." In another study (1969: 973) he correlates the attitudes uncovered in the survey with Russett's (1966) voting groups: the attitude of delegates from nations voting with the "Western Community" will be negative and static, whereas the attitudes of delegates from nations voting with the "Brazzaville Africans," "Afro-Asians," and "Communist bloc" will be positive and dynamic.

PROPOSITION 85: *The status of two nations is directly related to the trade between them.*
Reinton (1967: 343) has studied this proposition for eleven Latin American nations comprising 55 dyads for the early 1960s. The lower the average status of the nations in a dyad, the lower the trade level between them. If there is status discrepancy between the two nations, the greater the discrepancy, the stronger is the domination of one of the nations in their trade interactions. This domination is expressed in terms of the dominant nation limiting its partner's trade with others. These relationships also become manifest in patterns of influence. When the members of a pair are equal in status, each unit is capable of influencing the other's behavior when there is equilibrium in trade interactions.

The proposition seems to hold for certain systems, but not for others. Economic interaction between the NATO countries and the Warsaw Pact countries is highest between nations of large size and power, less between a nation of large size and power and one of small size and power, and least between two nations of small size and power (Galtung, 1966: 154-168). But in the Arab subsystem, the ranking of two nations in terms of status is not related to trade interaction (Thompson, 1970: 158).

PROPOSITION 86: *There is a relationship between a nation's status in the international system and its diplomatic interactions with other nations in terms of bilateral and multilateral contact.*
Nations interact in the traditional way of bilateral diplomatic exchanges between nations, or in the more recent way

of contact within an intergovernmental organization. Both of these types of interaction are rank-dependent.

Russett and Lamb (1969: 45), in a study of 104 nations for 1963-1964, observe that "by far the highest levels of diplomatic representation occur among the great powers, and within that group between great powers who are essentially allied with each other rather than hostile." Diplomatic interaction between NATO countries and Warsaw Pact countries for the period 1941-1965 tends to be rank-dependent according to Galtung (1966: 154-168). But not so for the Arab states in 1965: Thompson (1970: 158) finds no relationship between status rank and a limited form of diplomatic interaction, state visits.

Turning to diplomatic contact between nations in intergovernmental organizations, we find that, among all European nations not members of the Warsaw Pact plus non-European NATO countries, interaction in IGOs, NGOs, and business NGOs is stratified according to the wealth of the individual nations (Arosalo, 1970: 252). Among the five Nordic countries, personal interactions in the Fifth Committee of the U.N. were related to a different measure of status; these interactions were highest in central dyads, lower in central-periphery dyads, and lowest in periphery dyads (Kalela, 1967: 146). The broadest study relevant to this proposition, covering 115 nations in two periods (1950-1954, 1961-1962), comes to this conclusion:

low strata states shared a large number of IGO memberships with states in the other two strata. Middle strata states shared very few IGO memberships with other states. High strata states occupied a position between the other two strata in this regard [East, 1969: 127].

PROPOSITION 87:　*The Cold War system determines the linkages between states.*

Hopmann (1967: 231) studies the cohesion of the Communist system between 1950 and 1965: the U.S.S.R., China, and seven East European Warsaw Pact members. His finding is that "the greater the degree of East-West tension, the greater the degree of cohesion within the Communist system." Hoadley and Hasegawa (1971: 154), in their research on China and Japan, conclude that effective linkages are harder to establish between Cold War "enemies" and easier to establish between Cold War "allies."

Three studies relate Cold War tensions to trade linkages. In a longitudinal analysis of seven coutries between 1948 and 1962, Smoker (1965: 167) finds that Cold War tensions and trade are negatively related; his study concludes that trade is a very sensitive indicator of international relations. Russett (1967: 155) states that most of the changes in trading patterns in 1954 and 1963 can be attributed to movement into or out of the East European or Communist trading group. Finally, Smoker (1967: 69-71) finds that the greater the escalation of defense expenditures, the lower the trade between states, except for the dyads of USSR/Poland, USSR/China, and USA/China. Smoker's study is broader than this, however: he finds this same negative relationship for the tense period before the first World War. But, before the second world war, a negative relationship held for eventual adversaries and a positive relationship held for eventual allies.

PROPOSITION 88:   *The less the geographic distance between nations, the greater the interactions between them.*

Cobb and Elder (1970: 134) present the most general finding relevant to this proposition. In their analysis of 210 dyads in the North Atlantic region (1952-1964) and 1,176 dyads in the global system (1955), they find a positive relationship between geographic proximity and mutual relevance, especially in dyads where a common boundary is involved. The relationship holds for the global system, but not for the North Atlantic system. Brams (1966: 889) studied three specific types of interaction in his research on over 100 nations for the years 1962-1964. He finds that geographic proximity is one of the two most dominating influences in structuring the transaction flow subgroups for trade, diplomatic exchanges, and shared IGO memberships. Kegley studies interaction in terms of the types of acts nations direct at each other. Using the WEIS data for 452 dyads between 1966 and 1969, Kegley (1971: 365) finds that geographic distance is related to the acts nations direct at each other, but more so when those acts are "affective" than when they are "participatory."

Deutsch (1960b: 48) presents the only disconfirming finding on this proposition. Like Cobb and Elder, his research covers 15 North Atlantic nations (1890, 1913, 1938, 1954) and 106 nations in the global system (1938, 1954). His conclusion is that "geographic proximity has only limited effects on the distribution of international trade."

Rittberger (1971: 113) modifies this proposition when he controls for level of industrial technology. Studying 17 regional groupings in the mid-1960s, he finds that at lower levels of industrial technology, geographical distance is negatively related to multinational cooperation, but at higher levels distance is not an obstacle. With increasing communication between nations, geographical distance can be expected to exert less and less influence on all kinds of interactions.

PROPOSITION 89:   *The less the social and economic distance between nations, the greater the interactions between them.*

Of the 1,176 dyads studied by Cobb and Elder (1970: 135), those that are more homogeneous with respect to average developmental level will have greater mutual relevance. This tendency is especially pronounced for the most economically powerful dyads in the system. In addition, the more homogeneous two nations are in social welfare, the greater will be their level of interaction. Kegley (1971: 365), although he uses different variables in his study of 452 dyads (1966-1969), generally supports Cobb and Elder by finding that the degree of sociopolitical homogeneity between two nations is positively related to the "participatory," and more so to the "affective" behavior they direct at each other.

Where Cobb and Elder measure mutual relevance, Rummel (1969: 238) uses a similar measure called "salience"–the importance of one nation to another. His findings, though, are opposite: "The farther apart two nations are in their economic development and size, the more *salient* each is to the other (e.g., the more treaties, translations, tourists, etc.)."

PROPOSITION 90:   *The less the distance between nations in terms of governmental attributes, the greater the interaction between them.*

Several different governmental variables have been correlated to the overall flow of interactions among nations. The theoretical significance of this and the previous propositions may be limited, however. Correlating distance on different variables to interactions is a vacuous exercise without a theory that explains why a relationship is expected.

Cobb and Elder (1970: 135) find that for 1,176 dyads in the global system of 1955, those that are militarily more powerful exhibit somewhat greater mutual relevance; the relationship is moderate at best. Kegley (1971: 365) also finds only a moderate relationship; his variables are economic and military equality are "affective" and "participatory" behavior. The relationship is stronger for "affective" behavior. In Rittberger's research (1971: 113) on 17 regional groupings, equality in terms of power potential is more conducive to organized multinational cooperation.

As we noted in Chapter V, there has been little research focusing on the influence of bureaucratic capabilities on foreign policy-making. Similarly, there is only one study that looks at the difference in bureaucratic capabilities between two nations. Cobb and Elder (1970: 135) report a positive relationship between similarity in terms of bureaucratic capabilities and interaction. Another of their findings using govermental variables is the following: Nations with common historical attributes in terms of age and general stability but with dissimilar colonial experience show a slight tendency toward greater mutual relevance in the global system."

Finally, in Rummel's (1969b: 237) summary of the Dimensionality of Nations Project, he reports a positive relationship between similarity on the major attribute dimensions and transactions between two nations.

PROPOSITION 91: *The activities of the great powers limit the attempts of smaller states to maintain neutrality and independence.*

Even though the foreign policy of one major power may be directed only at other major powers, these activities indirectly affect smaller states. This is especially true in wartime. For five neutral nations in World War II, their boundaries of action were generally set by the relative military strength of the belligerents; the demands upon these neutral states depended upon relations between the belligerents, and not on any interest in the small states per se (Fox, 1959: 183). But in response, small nations do not arm themselves in defense against possible intrusions by any of the major powers. Instead, at least in the Cold War, small nations have become very cautious about arms escalation, for fear that they might be dragged into a war involuntarily (Jensen, 1969b: 322).

This question of dragging neutrals into war has been studied by Richardson (1960: xii) in his research on over 300 deadly quarrels between 1820 and 1945. The larger the number of belligerents involved in war, the more neutral states are drawn in. And if two major world powers are fighting each other, there is a greater likelihood that neutrals will evnetually take sides and become belligerents. As smaller states are eliminated in such situations either by voluntary union or by conquest, the balance of power system weakens (Wright, 1964: 126).

There are conditions that increase the neutral's chances of resisting the pressures of the great powers (Fox, 1959: 183-184):

(1) The more numerous the great powers with conflicting demands who are concerned about the small power and who could give effect to their concern—i.e., the more complex the balance.

(2) The more equal the balance of military strength among the contending great powers in the region of the small state.

(3) The greater the range of competing interests elsewhere on which the demanding great power needed to focus.

(4) The greater the distance the small state was located from a direct line between belligerents.

(5) The larger the quantity of scarce commodities or services useful for war purposes which the small state controlled and the more critical the scarcity to one or both sides.

(6) The larger the number of small states.

Competition among the great powers, though it may bring small states into thy conflict, may also provide small states with a means of influence (Vital, 1971: 124). In research on the Middle East crisis between May 16 and July 21, 1967, Young (1968: 71) concludes: "In general, it is the very political competition between the superpowers which allows the lesser powers to gain influence beyond their physical capacities by bartering their political orientations and allegiances." This relationship between great and small powers does not carry over into the United Nations. Lidstrom and Wiklund (1967: 185) analyze the votes of the five Nordic nations in 362 roll calls in the General Assembly, First Committee, and Special Political Committee for the years 1956-1965. They find no correlation between the unity of the superpowers in each session and the voting cohesion of the Nordic countries.

PROPOSITION 92:   *The policies of international organizations constrain the foreign policy activities of nations.*

In some cases, but certainly not in all, it can be said that international governmental organizations (IGOs) influence a state to do something that it might not otherwise do. But in those cases in which an IGO does not have this power, it can at least be said that the policies of IGOs are a factor that must be considered in foreign policy-making. Haas' research (1968: xxxiv) on the European Coal and Steel Community shows that the organization exerted pressure on its members to defer to its decisions lest their recalcitrance set a precedent for other governments. Looking at African interaction with the International Telegraph Union, the International Labor Organization, and the World Health Organization, Jacobsen (1970: 79) demonstrates that the more narrow and technical an organization, the less likely that broad political efforts of states (such as an attempt to exclude South Africa from membership) will succeed.

Can international organizations influence states in conflict situations in an attempt to maintain peace? In his research on 45 conflicts in the twentieth century, Wright (1965: 442) answers yes: a strong world opinion, manifested in international organization, demanding a cease-fire, negotiation, or renunciation of cause will tend to keep conflicts from escalating.

The United Nations has constrained the great powers from using the organization to pursue their own interests. Because of the influx of African states, the attention of the organization has shifted to issues of self-determination, economic and social development, and the elimination of colonialism (Hovet, 1963: 215).

Miscellaneous Findings

One of Rummel's studies (1967a: 182) focuses on the variable of "date of war" in 211 dyadic conflicts between 1820 and 1952. His conclusion is that date of war shows a slight positive relationship to intensity of violence for conflict between groups in general, but it is negatively related to intensity for nations only. The number of participants in war is also a factor; wars with many participants have tended to be longer and less frequent (Richardson, 1960: xii).

Singer and Small (1966: 18) have identified 112 formal agreements and 1,744 "war performance opportunities" involving 82 nations between 1815 and 1939. They find that of all nations, allied or not, the major powers showed the lowest propensity to remain neutral, the central system members fall in the intermediate position, and the total system members show the highest propensity to remain neutral.

Luard's comparison (1967: 173-176) of the interwar and postwar periods shows that the existence of homogeneous blocs which could integrate their strategies, as well as the ability of the members of the blocs to bring forces to bear on short notice, contributed to the adoption by nations of the general strategy of deterrence that has characterized military policy.

Two studies have looked at relations among allied nations. Examining NATO and the Warsaw Pact nations between 1961 and 1965, Galtung (1966: 153-154) reports that disparity between nations in terms of national attributes related to size and power results in conflict within an alliance. In a comparative case study of the French-American alliance and the Soviet-Chinese alliance since World War II, Holsti and Sullivan (1969: 166-167) find that the nature of the alliance is related to behavioral spillover. In a monolithic alliance, successful nonconforming alliance behavior of a member nation in one area tends to spill over into other issue-areas; but in a more pluralistic alliance, such spillover is limited.

In his research on foreign-linked factionalism in four historical periods, Dowty (1971: 433-435) uses several systemic variables and reports the following findings: foreign-linked factionalism is not related to the presence of a common border; neither is it related to the structure of the international system in terms of the isolation of conflicts and the "indirectness" of conflicts (those caused by membership in coalitions, financial inducements, and so on). But there is a significant negative relationship between foriegn-linked factionalism and the military equality of two states in all four time periods studied.

Russett (1968a) reaches the following conclusion in a diachronic analysis of world trading patterns:

The patterns of interdependence in 1938 will be less like those for 1954 than 1954 is like 1963 because:

(a) The time elapsed is greater, and changes in commercial habits are to some degree a function of time.

(b) Political changes on the Eurasian continent, specifically the communization of Eastern Europe and China, have cut old trading bonds and created different ones.

(c) Decolonization has weakened the bonds among the former British and French colonial empires.

(d) The physical damage and economic disruptions of World War II left much of the world, especially Europe, with a severe "dollar shortage" in the first postwar decade. As a consequence, Europeans' links to former markets and sources of supply outside their political spheres of influence were gravely weakened.

In addition, the patterns of trade interdependence in 1938 are less like those for 1963 and 1963 is like 1954 because of factors (a) - (c) above. Factor (d) no longer operated in 1963. The patterns of trade interdependence in 1938 are neither more nor less similar to 1963 than they are to 1954.

The existence of economic organizations in a regional system forces nonmembers to cooperate economically. In an analysis of fifteen nations in the North Atlantic area between 1928 and 1963, Alker and Puchala (1968: 315) find a "noticeable increase in the normally weak economic partnerships among non-EEC countries in the postwar era."

Finally, Tanter (1966: 62), in his study of 83 nations for the years 1958-1960, makes this statement: "Level of world interest in a nation is associated with the tendency for its protests and expulsions of ambassadors to be reported."

Evaluation

The major criticism of the research included in this chapter focuses on the propositions which have interaction as the dependent variable. The many studies relating distance on various attributes to interactions are very diverse, and there has been no attempt at replication. Before we can build general theory, we must be able to formulate specific propositions connecting distance on one attribute to one kind of interaction.

The only propositions that we have some confidence in are Propositions 79, 80, 83, 86, and 88. All of these employ specific variables and are supported by several works. Clearly, more research needs to be done on the influence of the international system upon foreign policy. In this fashion linkages can be built between the findings of specialists in international relations and those in foreign policy studies.

NOTE

1. James N. Rosenau, "Pre-Theories and Theories of Foreign Policy," pp. 65-71 in R. B. Farrell (ed.) *Approaches to Comparative and International Politics* (Evanston, Ill.: Northwestern University Press, 1966).

Chapter XIV

DECISION-MAKING VARIABLES

Having completed our consideration of the independent variable categories, both internal and external to the nation-state, we turn now to the intervening variable cluster of decision-making. Classified under this category are such factors as the value screen of the individual, the information available to decision-makers, the goals guiding a policy, the perceptions and expectations of decision-makers, the level of risk involved in a decision, the costs of a decision, and the nature of the issue. As described in the Introduction and diagrammed in Figure 5, these kinds of variables may modify the impact of the independent variables on foreign policy output.

The reader will notice that many of the propositions presented in this section are not really propositions at all, in the sense that they do not relate a decision-making variable to the dependent variable of foreign policy output. The major weakness of the few comparative studies that examine decision-making variables is that they just show that an independent variable is operative, but do not demonstrate how it operates in the foreign policy process. Nevertheless, we decided to include these one-variable statements in the inventory because: (1) they can serve as the basis for future hypothesis-testing, and (2) "they're all we've got."

PROPOSITION 93:   *The value screen of the decision-maker affects his nation's foreign policy output.*

The first study reported in this section is a good example of these shortcomings. Choucri (1969b: 72) tries to identify elements of the value screen of leaders, but does not relate these elements to a dependent variable. Her findings are based on a content analysis of speeches at the conferences in Bogor (1954), Bandung (1955), and Belgrade (1961) by three nonaligned leaders—Sukarno, Nehru, and Nasser. These leaders view the actions of major powers in clearly negative terms, but they do not transfer these negative attitudes to international alignments or to the international system in general. There does not seem to be any difference between their evaluations of East and West in terms of affect, potency, and activity, although there are some discrepancies in the activity dimension (Choucri, 1969a: 8-9; 1969b: 72). Nor do these leaders see the capabilities of East and West or their actions toward the nonaligned nations as different. Corresponding to these perceptions and evaluations of other nations as similar, the nonaligned nations treat East and West in a similar manner. Choucri (1969a: 11-14) placed 500 foreign policy acts taken from *Deadline Data* and other sources along a cooperative-conflictual scale and found that the three nations taken together treat East and West similarly; but when she examined them individually, she found that Egypt was more conflictual toward the West and more cooperative to the East, while India and Indonesia displayed the opposite pattern.

Is the value screen of the foreign policy decision-maker

derived from the domestic political system, from other nations, or from the international system? Hanrieder (1967: 232) tries to answer this question in his diachronic study of West Germany. His conclusion is that foreign policy objectives have been formulated in terms of a combination of internal, external, and systemic referents.

PROPOSITION 94: *In crisis situations, decision-makers of opposing nations tend to have similar perceptions.*

Holsti, North, and Brody have studied this proposition with respect to the decision-makers of five nations in the six weeks prior to World War I. In a two-step, mediated stimulus-response (S-r: s-R) model, they find (1968: 157) no significant difference between the members of the Dual Alliance and the Triple Entente in regard to the r-s link or the s-R link. However, they do find a significant difference between the two coalitions in regard to the S-r link, with the leaders of the Dual Alliance overperceiving the actions of the opponent, and the leaders of the Triple Entente underperceiving the actions of their opponent. Generally, each nation saw itself as the agent of friendship and the target of undeserved hostility, and saw its enemies as agents of hostility and targets of friendship. (Holsti and North, 1965: 167). This type of perceptual screen was most operative at key points in the prewar crisis when leaders were making crucial policy decisions.

These findings of general similarity of perceptions are confirmed by a study of another crisis. In a content analysis of 96 documents from five Israeli and five Egyptian decision-makers during the 1956-1957 Suez crisis, Silverson (1970: 165) finds that decision-makers "tend to perceive their own nation as the target of high levels of injury." He also finds that leaders of both countries perceived the U.N. as a target of injury, though at fluctuating levels.

Schwartz's study focuses not on perceptions of injury or of actions, but on perceptions of the costs of a crisis. One of the conclusions (1967: 485) of his analysis of eight Soviet-

American crises between 1950 and 1964 is that "in almost every crisis, for both sides, there is a tendency for perceived costs to rise—suggesting that crises may be an inefficient means of conducting foreign relations."

Zaninovitch traces the changes in perceptions of events of different decision-makers from a noncrisis to a crisis situation. Analyzing the official newspapers of the Soviet Union and Communist China for January 1960 and May 1960, Zaninovitch (1962: 265) finds a change in the statements of leaders of both countries from relative friendliness and nonviolence and unconcern about impending change to feelings of animosity and intense emotion and great concern about impending change.

Do decision-makers have similar perceptions in noncrisis situations? This question has been dealt with in two studies. Eckhardt and White (1967: 331), in research on the speeches of Kennedy (1961-1963) and Kruschchev (1961), conclude that the two leaders were not significantly different from each other on five indices of conflict-mindedness. Nor were they different in expressed value judgments, being "equally aggressive in defending their own nation's sovereignty, and equally denunciatory of each other's aggression, dominance, and immorality in general."

Jervis (1968: 475), in a nonsystematic analysis of decision-makers in various situations, finds that actors tend "to see other states as more hostile than they are" and they "tend to see the behavior of others as more centralized, disciplined, and coordinated than it is." In addition, Jervis (1968: 476) reports that:

actors tend to overestimate the degree to which others are acting in response to what they themselves do when the others behave in accordance with the actor's desires; but when the behavior of the other is undesired, it is usually seen as derived from internal forces.

PROPOSITION 95:   *The "mood" of a nation affects its foreign policy activity.*

Klingberg, in an early study, has tried to scientifically delineate the "mood" of a nation—a factor so often cited in the speeches of politicians. His analysis covers eight cycles of American foreign policy between 1776 and 1950. He finds (1952: 240-260) that there has been a regular alternation in the "mood" of American foreign policy behavior between introversion and extroversion; these cycles have lasted two decades or more and alternation has occurred before three decades have passed. Such periods can be measured by the percentages (in lines or words) of State of the Union addresses, inaugural addresses, and political party platforms devoted to descriptions of, or demands for, positive action abroad. And they become manifest in the rates of increase in annual naval expenditures of the government.

PROPOSITION 96: *The source and the nature of communications affect the perception of, and receptivity to, messages from other nations.*

This and the next two propositions have been studied only by Jervis, in a nonsystematic analysis of various "actors" in international politics. Concerning the source of communications, Jervis (1968: 473) finds that "when messages are sent from a different background of concerns and information than is possessed by the receiver, misunderstanding is likely." He also reports (1968: 476) that "because a state gets most of its information about the other state's policies from the other's foreign office, it tends to take the foreign office's position for the stand of the other government as a whole." Concerning the nature of communications, Jervis (1968: 465) finds that "actors can more easily assimilate into their established image of another actor information contradicting that image if the information is transmitted and considered bit by bit than if it comes all at once."

PROPOSITION 97: *The ties which a decision-maker has to existing theories and images affect his perceptions and expectations.*

Jervis (1968: 459) finds that the mistakes of decision-makers are definitely the result, not of being too willing to alter existing theories, but of being too tied to established theories and thus closed to new information. The theory structures the information being received, especially if this information is ambiguous or if the theory is held with a great deal of confidence (1968: 455). Thus, the environment may be misperceived, and Jervis (1968: 467) finds that "misperception is most difficult to correct in the case of a missing concept and least difficult to correct in the case of a recognized but presumably unfilled concept."

The ties which a decision-maker has to existing images or theories have two other effects (Jervis, 1968: 478). "Actors tend to overlook the fact that evidence consistent with their theories may also be consistent with other views." And it is difficult for the actor "to see that issues important to him are not important to others."

PROPOSITION 98:   *Decision-makers often do not realize that their intentions and actions are not perceived as they expected them to be.*

Jervis (1968: 474, 477) presents three findings relevant to this proposition. "When actors have intentions that they do not try to conceal from others, they tend to assume that others accurately perceive these intentions. . . . When people spend a great deal of time drawing up a plan or making a decision, they tend to think that the message about it they wish to convey will be clear to the receiver." Finally, he reports that "actors often do not realize that actions intended to project a given image may not have the desired effect because the actions themselves do not turn out as planned."

PROPOSITION 99:   *Foreign policy-makers try to minimize the risk in their actions.*

On the basis of the influence of one or more of the independent variables in our framework, a decision-maker might formulate a particular course of action. But then when he considers the risk involved in that action, he might change his plans. The modifying influence of risk has been shown to be operative in crisis situations. Holsti, Brody, and North (1969: 693) find that in the Cuban missile crisis of 1962, Soviet and American decision-makers were always consciously concerned with choosing acts at the lowest level of violence or potential violence necessary to achieve their goals. And Schwartz's study (1967: 484) of the same two nations in eight crises shows that risk-taking is patterned and quite consistent across time in similar circumstances: decision-makers prefer "alternatives with lower gains but also lower costs and risks to policies promising greater benefits at higher cost and risk levels."

When a nation's leaders are considering violent foreign policy action, there is a minimum to which risks can be reduced, in crisis or in noncrisis situations. That is, most violent decisions are taken without adequate information, so that there is always a relatively high level of risk, despite decision-makers' attempts to minimize it (Haas, 1969a: 86).

PROPOSITION 100: *Foreign policy-makers' goals account for the distribution of their nation's foreign aid.*

Wittkopf's research (1971: 102) on the aid given by the members of the Development Assistance Committee between 1961 and 1967 shows that only U.S. aid can be accounted for in terms of Cold War security objectives. This pursuit of Cold War objectives has been studied by Tansky (1967: 177) in a comparison of Soviet and American aid to India, Turkey, and the U.A.R.; his conclusion is that the use of aid as a weapon in the Cold War has diminished the effect of that aid upon economic development. As for the goals of other DAC donors, both Wittkopf (1971, abstract: 3) and Vellut (1967: 263) find that the political importance of the recipient accounts for the distribution of aid; Wittkopf further finds that need of foreign exchange support and self-interest as reflected in trade ties are explanatory goals. Walters (1970:

47) looks at Soviet and American goals in more general terms and finds that the distribution of aid results from the pursuit of milieu goals by these two nations.

Two findings modify Proposition 100: Walters (1970: 68-69) finds that the professed goals of aid donors—for the U.S., political and economic development; and for the U.S.S.R., the spread of the revolution—have been more operative in the type and content of aid than in the selection of the countries which are to receive it. And Tansky (1967: 168-171) finds that there is often little relationship between stated U.S. policy objectives and the distribution of its aid, but more connection between Soviet objectives and distribution.

What are the goals that guide the cutting off of aid and other economic flows through sanctions? Wallensteen's research (1968: 262) on eighteen and ten cases of sanctions between 1933 and 1967 shows that "the sender's motive in general has been to express feelings after the receiver has broken norms fundamental to the sender."

PROPOSITION 101: *The goals of foreign policy-makers are related to the demands made upon other states.*

McKenna (1962: 196), in his analysis of five American diplomatic protests, tries to relate goals to the formulation of those protests. He finds that the pursuit of objectives not related to its prima facie demands has *not* been a factor in the formulation of protests. Also, ulterior motives have been more influential in anticipating the costs of protests than in formulating the aims.

Goals can be related to the demands made on another state for social change. The research by Ness (1969: 60-62) on five cases of land reform shows that the demands of the superordinate nation can have a decisive effect on social change in a subordinate nation when those demands are concerned with effecting basic changes, making them diffuse and profound.

There are, of course, demands made upon recipient nations

when aid is donated. Walters (1970: 169) relates goals to these demands in finding that

since the U.S.S.R. seems less concerned than the United States with an attempt to combat systematically the problems of economic development in the less developed countries, there is less need for the Soviet Union to make aid conditional upon basic internal reforms and economic performance by the recipient.

Walters also finds (1970: 119) that the goal of economic development accounts for the activist relationship between the U.S. and recipient countries in administration of that aid, while the goal of establishing a political and economic presence accounts for the passive relationship between the U.S.S.R. and recipients.

Goals can also account for the success of demands on other states, at least in the area of coercion. George, Hall and Simons (1971: 216) demonstrate in their comparative case studies of Laos, Cuba, and Vietnam that the success of U.S. coercive diplomacy is partially dependent on the clarity of American objectives and a sense of urgency to achieve the objectives that is perceived by the other side, on the strength of U.S. motivation and an asymmetry of motivation favoring the U.S., and on clarity concerning the precise demands and terms of settlement.

PROPOSITION 102: *The nature of the issue affects voting in the United Nations.*

Most of the comparative research that is issue-specific focuses on U.N. voting, probably because the "issue" is easily defined when it is manifest in a pattern of votes. Lidstrom and Wiklund study the proposition for the five Nordic nations on 362 roll calls in the General Assembly, First Committee, and Special Political Committee between 1956 and 1965. Kalela studies the proposition for the Nordic nations on 1470 (unspecified) roll calls between 1956 and 1966. Lidstrom and Wiklund (1967: 186) find that the general level of activity of these nations in the U.N. varies with the nature of the issue, with disarmament questions producing the most activity. Both articles report that cohesion among the five nations depends on the issue involved (Lidstrom and Wiklund, 1967: 186; Kalela, 1967: 168). More specifically, the lower the power politics content of an issue, the higher the cohesion; and the higher the supranationalism content of an issue, the higher the cohesion (Kalela, 1967: 168).

Jacobsen (1967: 151-152) studies the effect of the nature of the issue on the voting alignment of Nordic countries with the West. His analysis treats the 1946-1953 period diachronically. One finding is that "though the Nordic countries are clearly on the side of the West on questions defined as East-West issues, this is less true of the later periods than before." The other finding is that for all Nordic countries except Finland, "increasing degrees of conflict [in East-West issues] results in increasing agreement with the West, but in the case of Sweden the increase is very low, while Iceland shows the highest rate followed by Norway and Denmark."

Two studies focus on the relationship of issue to the activity of African states in the United Nations. Kay's analysis (1969: 44) of the period 1955-1968 reports that African states tend to abstain or absent themsevles on votes connected with the East-West conflict, for involvement in this conflict is seen as irrelevant to their own goals and a danger to achievement of those goals. Hovet's analysis (1963: 225) of the period 1946-1962 reports that "whereas the African caucusing group has increased its ability to negotiate by stressing its primary interest in. African issues, the Casablanca group, in broadening its concerns, has in many instances lost its ability to negotiate."

PROPOSITION 103: *The nature of the issue affects the foreign policy activity of states.*

Only three studies have tested this important theoretical proposition, so the dependent variable cannot yet be made more specific. Touval's work (1966: 646) on seven border disputes in Africa in the 1960s finds that the nature of the issue is related to the solution of those disputes. The amount of teritory involved is directly proportional to the intractability of the dispute. And an issue's position along a continuum of ideological versus technical content and along a continuum of vital national interest versus marginal national interest is directly proportional to the intractability of the dispute. Holsti's content analysis (1970: 305) of the statements of decision-makers involved' in the pre-World War I crisis shows that differences between situations (i.e., issues) are more related to perceptions of hostility than are differences among individuals within a nation. Finally, McKenna (1962: 195), in his work on five American diplomatic protests, shows that nations respond more readily to those protests which involve established international usages carrying assurance of reciprocal treatment, as in cases concerned with diplomatic and consular immunities.

PROPOSITION 104: *The longer the time taken in formulating a policy decision, the more alternatives will be considered and the more rational will be the process.*

In an historical study of 25 major wars in modern history, Abel (1941: 855) reports that the decision to go to war is reached one to five years before the outbreak of hostilities. The consequence is that officials undertake a careful weighing of the relevant factors and the anticipated consequences of actions, so that decisions are not taken on the basis of emotional tensions, sentimentality, crowd behavior, or other irrational motivations. Haas (1969a: 86) agrees, basing his conclusions on research on violent foreign policy in the twentieth century. War is undertaken, he states, when officials have long been concerned with hostility between nations and have long recognized the target as an enemy. In this long period the number of violent options considered is high, and foreign policy becomes a maximizing more than a satisficing choice, in accordance with the rationality model of decision-making.

An exception to Abel's finding was the first World War; decision-makers did not expect war to break out at the time, and the prewar crisis escalated so quickly that rational policy making on the decision to go to war was limited. North (1967: 116, 118) finds that "at almost every major turning point, the men who made the crucial decisions were strongly affected by essentially emotional, non-rational phenomena."

PROPOSITION 105: *The greater the demands on the decision-making apparatus, the more likely it is that violent foreign policy will result.*

In France, Germany, Japan, and the United States, the decision-making framework is one of six variable groups that show a small to moderate relationship with military control of foreign policy (Benjamin and Edinger, 1971: 14). More specifically, when foreign policy issues make large demands on the society's resources, it is more likely that the military will control foreign policy.

Smoker (1969: 187-188) has used decision-making variables in a longitudinal analysis of Sino-Indian relations between 1959 and 1964. Before the crisis over the Dalai Lama incident in Tibet in 1960, the demands on the decision systems of the two nations were limited. This meant that freedom of decision was never lost by both nations at once, "lock-in" was avoided, and information overload was not apparent. Consequently, the crisis did not break down into war. Before the border crisis between India and China in 1962, however, freedom of decision was restricted for both sides, a "lock-in" situation occurred, and there was an information overload. The result was that the crisis led to war.

Miscellaneous Findings

Small and Singer (1970: 151) report that time of the year was a factor in the outbreak of war during the 121-year period they studied. Over two-thirds of all wars started in the spring or autumn; however, time of the year is not related to the termination of war.

Decision-making capability may be a factor limiting the number of states with which a nation can interact. Kegley's research (1971: 365) on 452 dyads from 1966 to 1969 reports that nations concentrate their foreign policy attention on a relatively small number of targets.

The effect of the foreign policy tool used has been a neglected area of research. Only two studies consider this variable. McKenna (1962: 198) reports that the United States has avoided the use of active sanctions because leaders have regarded them as unfeasible, inefficacious, and/or too expensive. Walters (1970: 147) notes that there is more than one way to achieve objectives: flexibility and quickness of implementation in economic aid programs are achieved by the U.S. through a wide variety of formal, specialized mechanisms; while the Soviet Union achieves these objectives through the small size and the informality of its mechanisms.

Evaluation

We have already stated our major criticism of the studies in this section: much of the research shows that a decision-making variable is operative, but does not examine the effect of that variable on foreign policy output. Another criticism is that the research ignores some of the key decision-making variables, namely the amount of information available to the decision-maker and the costs of the decision. Part of the blame for this neglect lies with the theoretical literature, which has paid far too little attention to specifying the types of and the nature of the decision-making variables important for comparative studies of foreign policy.

In spite of this neglect, we do have the beginnings of knowledge in this area. It seems clear that opposing decision-makers tend to have similar perceptions in a crisis (Proposition 94). The influence of goals in accounting for certain types of foreign policy has been pretty well validated

(Propositions 100 and 101). The role of the nature of the issue (Proposition 102) has been well substantiated, at least in U.N. voting (although the analyses should be extended to wider groups of nations); but research on the influence of this factor in other activity is limited.

Chapter XV

THE FEEDBACK PROCESS

Throughout this inventory we have been concerned with the causes of foreign policy behavior, and have paid little attention to the consequences of that behavior. Yet it is at least as important to know what the impact of an act is as it is to know what caused that act. The two feedback loops in Figure 5 are a conceptual device to enable the researcher to fit behavioral consequences into the foreign policy decision-making process. One loop, which will be treated first in this section, indicates the impact of foreign policy acts on the actor itself; it includes impact on domestic politics and on other foreign policies. The other loop indicates that a nation's acts affect the politics of the international system.

PROPOSITION 106: *Variations in the external environment over time affect the domestic politics of a nation.*

When nations engage in foreign conflict and there is a rise in tension in the external environment, the domestic economy is soon affected. This was quite evident in the six weeks prior to World War I. The virtual collapse of prices during that period can be attributed to rising international tensions (Holsti, North, and Brody, 1968: 145). Likewise, other indicators of economic conditions were affected by the intensity of perceived hostility in the pre-war crisis: the daily average net flow of gold in and out of London, fluctuations in the prices of stocks and bonds, fluctuations in the exchange rate for British pounds and in bank interest rates, and changes in the prices of commodity futures (Holsti, North, and Brody, 1968: 139; Holsti and North, 1970: 131; Holsti and North, 1966: 175-184.

Wright (1964: 219) finds a positive relationship between international tension and the intensity of nationalism expressed by societies. Chadwick (1969: 209), in a study using the DON data on 64 nations for 1955, finds that the greater (i.e., the lower the international tension) national security, the greater the likelihood of revolution.

Cohen (1969: 131) finds a varying relationship between the two variables of this proposition:

Whereas the Cold War environment seems to play a greater role in United States politics and political strategies than in the Soviet Union, the regional environment seems to play a greater role in Soviet internal politics and political strategies than it does in the United States.

However, Cohen (1969: 139) reports that for both countries, there is little relationship between the nature of the international environment and the selection of leaders from particular social backgrounds.

The last several years have shown us that internal wars are no longer purely domestic matters, that the international environment has a major impact on such conflict. Modelski (1964: 147) is the only one who has studied this important type of penetration. In research on seven internal wars in the twentieth century, he concludes that "The outside world is the most efficient (though not the only) provider of third-party influence which, in turn, may be essential for achieving a stalemate and for building up the center."

Several kinds of environmental factors have facilitated the penetration of West Germany since World War II (Hanrieder, 1967: 233-236). Among these have been the agreement of European and American policy-makers on major policy concepts and the overwhelming influence of international contingencies. As penetration proceeds, the patterns of "compatibility" that relate goals to the external environment begin to overlap with the patterns of "consensus" that relate goals to the internal environment.

PROPOSITION 107: *The existence of linkages to other nations and linkage groups affects domestic politics and policy-making.*

In Chapter XI we were concerned with the effect of linkages with other countries on a nation's foreign policy. Here we will examine how those ties feed back onto the internal environment and affect domestic politics and policy-making. Chalmers (1969: 76-89) has done one of the few empirical studies on the subject of linkage politics, and it is his findings that are reported here. His analysis focuses on comparative case studies of various Latin American nations.

Linkages with external economies have retarded the growth of differentiated interest groups and have given rise to a paternalism in which different economic groups are dependent on the government (pp. 76-78). In accordance with this paternalism, demands are processed and conflicts resolved "through traditional informal means or through the more or less 'private' representation through the bureaucracy" (p. 89). There is, thus, an oligarchical system which is based on control of technology, finances, and trade from abroad and which allows the linkage elites to control the distribution of economic resources, social status, and the means of violence (p. 79). Much of the advice that comes from external actors has the effect of perpetuating this political situation (p. 84). In addition, the anticipation of the demands of foreign investment by bureaucracies appears to entail a reinforcement of the role of the leadership in a paternalist fashion, a great emphasis on the administration of reform, and the opportunity for elites who initiate and execute these reforms to manipulate them in such a way as to avoid serious threats to their position (p. 86-87).

The adoption of policies and institutions evolved in foreign contexts by Latin American linkage groups, along with the "demonstration effect" of other nations, has three results. First, it creates disillusionment with policy-makers and the possibilities of reform (p. 84). Second, it produces a rising level of demands, especially among the middle class (p. 78). And third, ideological conflict takes on the character of conflict in the rest of the world (p. 81).

Holt and Turner (1969: 211) apply the hypotheses of linkage politics to insular polities. In their comparative case study of Great Britain, Japan, Ceylon, and the Malagasy Republic, they conclude that "an insular polity may have a relatively large number of linkage groups, and these groups may have stronger ties to the domestic system" so that the "insular policy should react more frequently, more quickly, and more strongly to inputs from the international system." In order to reduce its dependence on, and avoid domination by, stronger states, the insular polity attempts to occupy sections of the mainland to avoid invasion of the island, maintain a balance of power among mainland polities, or call upon outside allies for support.

A final linkage study that we can examine is Ness' research (1969: 60-62) on five cases of land reform imposed on a nation. He finds that one of the conditions under which the foreign policy of a superordinate nation can control the goals of the subordinate nation is an abnormally close relationship between goals, allowing for direct intervention in major policy decisions.

PROPOSITION 108: *The occurence of external conflict behavior is positively related to internal conflict.*

Rummel (1964: 93) studies this proposition for 69 nations for 1955-1957 and for 66 nations for 1946-1959, correlating nine domestic and thirteen foreign conflict variables at one point in time. In one of his few positive statements he finds that

high foreign conflict behavior, in terms of such acts as severance of diplomatic relations, expulsion or recall of ambassadors and other diplomatic officials, negative sanctions, and military action, has a small but generally consistent relationship to the existence of general domestic conflict behavior.

His conclusion is supported by Otterbein's research (1968: 104-105) on fifty "so-called primitive or tribal societies." Otterbein finds a high positive correlation between external war and internal "feuding" in uncentralized political systems, but the opposite relationship in centralized political systems. However, he finds no relationship between external war and internal war in either type of system.

Tanter and Wilkenfeld both introduce a time lag in their research and their findings are mixed. Tanter (1966: 57), like Rummel, does not categorize either type of nation or type of conflict behavior, and he finds a weak positive relationship between the 1955-1957 foreign conflict and 1958-1960 domestic conflict of 83 nations. Wilkenfeld (1969: 153; 1971: 199-201) breaks down the 74 nations in his research into categories and factor analyzes domestic and foreign conflict for the years 1955 to 1960, with the following results: For polyarchic nations, foreign conflict behavior of any type is never followed by the domestic conflict factors "revolutionary" or "subversive." For centrist nations, foreign conflict behavior of any type is never followed by domestic conflict behavior of any type—a finding unique to the centrist group. For personalist nations, there are significant positive correlations between "diplomatic" conflict and internal "turmoil" at the same time and one year later, and between "belligerency" and "internal war" one and two years later.

PROPOSITION 109: *External events have little effect on public images.*

Despite the impact that the external environment has on domestic politics, it may not be able to shift the dominant images of a large segment of the public. Deutsch and Merritt (1965: 183) have studied 18 cases (1946-1963) from different countries in which events would be expected to change public images. They find that the most spectacular events in politics alter the images of only one-fifth to one-third of the population. The rare occasions where the images of 50 or 60 percent of the population are shifted "require the combination and mutual reinforcement of cumulative events with spectacular events and substantial government efforts as well as the absence of sizeable cross-pressures;" even when these conditions obtain, about 40 percent of the population will still not be affected. If these conditions do not obtain, the magnitude of opinion shifts declines to between 10 and 20 percent. However, over much longer periods of time, the cumulative impact of events has a much larger effect on public images.

If public attitudes do change in response to events, this change is more likely to take place in high education and interest (voting) groups. This is the finding of Rosi (1965: 293) in diachronic research on American citizens between 1954 and 1963.

PROPOSITION 110: *The foreign policy acts of a nation affect public opinion.*

Hero (1969: 233) studies this proposition in a diachronic analysis of the United States between 1937 and 1967. Using survey data from AIPO, Elmo Roper, NORC, and SRC, he finds that the recent transfer of aid from Europe to the less developed nations and the increased attention being given to Asia and Africa have been received somewhat more favorably among blacks than among whites. In another diachronic analysis of the U.S. (1954-1963), Rosi (1965: 296) finds that foreign policy influences, rather than is influenced by, public opinion. Specifically, his conclusion is that govern-mental changes in nuclear testing suspension preceded rather than followed changes in public opinion. Katz and Piret (1964: 369) analyze the Gallup polls at the time of the 1960 U-2 incident and the 1961 Bay of Pigs invation. Their interesting finding is that "patterns of increased *approval* follow actions by the President (or actions for which he is held accountable) that are clearly recognized as major errors, if not disasters—as independently reflected in newspapers." But this increased approval may be short-lived, as Mueller finds in a study of Truman, Eisenhower, Kennedy, and Johnson. He observes (1970: 28) a popularity decline of five or six percent for every year since what he calls the previous "rally point."

What is the effect of war on public opinion? Mueller's study (1970: 28) finds that "the Korean War had a large, significant, independent negative impact on President Tru-man's popularity of some 18 percentage points, but the Vietnam War had no independent impact on President Johnson's popularity at all." In another study that compares these two wars, Mueller (1971: 365-366) finds that the beginnings of the wars generated about the same amount of public support, and that it was not the events of the wars that diminished public support but the increasing number of casualities: "every time American casualities increased by a factor of 10 . . . support for the war dropped by about 15 percentage points." Mitchell (1971: 58) adds a qualification to these studies on the basis of his research on the Vietnam war. He finds that during periods of stress in the course of the war, public opinion support for President Johnson sharply increased, despite the general downward trend in support level. The American people have traditionally sup-ported their President when he acts in a crisis, though support is short-lived.

One explanation for the negative effect of war on public opinion is that people are affected personally by the nation's foreign policy. In research on 72 nations between 1958 and

1960, Haas (1969b: 278-279) finds a positive relationship between internal and external violence and the lowering of health standards within a nation. But he finds no relationship between conflict-related deaths and deaths due to other causes.

PROPOSITION 111: *The foreign policy acts of a nation affect party politics favorably for incumbent officials.*

Four quite different studies try to demonstrate the impact of foreign policy acts on party politics. Holsti and Sullivan's comparative analysis (1969: 155) of France and Communist China since World War II shows that "nonconforming alliance politics may serve to solidify the position of top leaders." Hoffmann's comparative analysis (1967: 154) of the League of Nations' sanctions against Italy in 1935 and the British sanctions against Rhodesia in 1965 reports that sanctions are effective in alleviating the tension on political leaders in a cross-pressure situation. The comparative study by Finlay, Holsti, and Fagen (1967: 179-181) of Castro, Dulles, and Nkrumah and other Ghanaian leaders shows that foreign enemies have been used by leaders, especially in Ghana, to create internal political unity. Finally, Hanrieder's diachronic analysis (1967: 237) of West Germany shows that "the early recognition that foreign policy would decisively shape the nature of the domestic political order necessarily led the SPD to direct its main thrusts against the foreign policy of the government." Hanrieder (1967: 243) also finds that the limits of what could be accomplished in the international system brought about a consensus among the German political parties on foreign policy, which then contributed to the decreased emphasis on ideology in domestic politics.

PROPOSITION 112: *The greater the level of foreign policy activity, the greater is the social and political growth of a nation.*

If we think of role conceptions as a factor in political growth, then Holsti's research (1970: 283-284) on 71 states is relevant to this proposition. He content analyzes the statements of top decision-makers, each of whom have a minimum of ten statements of role conceptions between January 1965 and December 1967. His conclusion is that the more active and involved a state is in the international system, the more highly structured are role conceptions and the more conceptions its leaders will perceive.

Activity in the international system is often related to the level of a nation's defense expenditures. Wolf (1965: 888, 890; 1967: 108-109), in diachronic analyses of twenty Latin American nations, correlates defense expenditures for the period 1950-1960 with the scores on level of political development from Fitzgibbon and Johnson (1961). He finds that defense expenditures have a moderate positive relationship with level of development (r_s = .46 and .40), but no significant relationship with change in level of development.

In contrast to defense expenditures, which boost an economy, war involvement is negatively related to socio-political development. Wright (1964: 166) finds that war involvement leads to rigid and unadaptive social institutions.

PROPOSITION 113: *The activities of intergovernmental organizations have speeded the social and economic growth of developing nations.*

Generally, the aid activities of intergovernmental organizations have worked. In Latin America, IGO assistance per capita between 1953 and 1961 is associated with lower level of civil violence in the period 1961-1963 (Tanter, 1970: 176). In Africa, the activities of IGOs have not only increased economic growth through money and material, but they have also influenced the development goals and programs adopted by African nations (Jacobsen, 1970: 92-93). In addition, IGOs have the political effect in Africa of encouraging tendencies towards pluralism when they aid the organization of labor, create new bureaucracies, and assist cooperative movements (Jacobsen, 1970: 93). And by keeping the Cold War from the continent, the U.N. has been able to promote social and economic development (Hovet, 1963: 215).

PROPOSITION 114: *Variations in foreign policy acts over time are related to each other.*

What is the effect of a particular foreign policy act on other acts? Are the different types of behavior of one nation interrelated? This question can be considered in terms of a feedback process. A number of diverse studies are related to it.

The most general finding is reported by Kegley (1971: 363). Analyzing the foreign policy behavior of 452 dyads coded in the WEIS data for the period January 1966 to August 1969, Kegley makes this statement: "Most types of acts which nations initiate toward one another are generally related to other kinds of acts; that is, they tend to co-occur in uniform patterns." Moreover, these foreign policy patterns are quite stable over time (Kegley, 1971: 363).

Rummel (1963: 24) confirms the proposition in a study of foreign conflict acts. In analysis of 77 nations for the years 1955-1957, he finds that "the variation in acts or occurrences of foreign conflict behavior are generally highly related to each other." Tanter's replication (1966: 61) of this study confirms its findings for the 1955-1957 period and reports a similar relationship, only somewhat weaker, for the 1958-1960 period. In addition, Tanter (1966: 55) introduces a time lag and finds that the 1955-1957 foreign conflict predicts 22.3 percent of the variance in the 1958-1960 foreign conflict. Weede's replication (1970: 231) also confirms Rummel, but with a modification. Weede studies the entire period 1955-1960 for 59 nations using the same DON data, but he dichotomizes conflict behavior and finds this relationship: "Verbal foreign conflict behavior of nations makes involvement in violent foreign conflict much more likely, whereas violent foreign confict has a minor feedback on verbal foreign conflict behavior only." Finally, when they control for level of domestic conflict, Zinnes and Wilkenfeld (1971: 184) support the other studies with their finding that for all types of nations, "the level of previous foreign conflict predicts the level of subsequent foreign conflict behavior."

Besides being associated with each other, foreign conflict acts are also associated with cooperative acts. This is the finding of Kegley's research (1971: 364): he states that the two types of behavior "tend to co-vary and be consistently associated with one another."

Can we predict who a nation will fight against on the basis of its enemies and friends in the past? The answer of Small and Singer (1970: 154) is negative. Nations that have fought once before are not more likely to fight again than nations that have never fought; likewise, nations that have not fought before are not more likely to remain friends than nations who have fought.

Does greater involvement in the international system show a positive feedback to involvement in foreign conflict? Rummel's work (1966b: 211) on 82 nations in the mid-1950s and Terrell's work (1972: 185) on 75 nations for the same period report that no such relationship exists. But East and Gregg (1967: 265), using the same (DON) data, find that the frequency of both cooperation and conflict tends to be greater for nations that are more involved in international activity.

Involvement in international activity has been correlated with behavior in the U.N. by both Alger and Rummel. Alger's observations (1968: 68-75) of 3,475 interactions among delegates in the Fifth Committee in 1962 show that such activity is moderately related to U.N. support in terms of committee attendance and number of men in the permanent mission and in the General Assembly, and to U.N. support in terms of voluntary contributions, contributions to the regular budget, and total U.N. contributions. But he does not find a significant rank correlation between interaction of a group and that group's voting agreement. Rummel (1969: 238), studying 164 and 182 dyads for 1955, finds that "U.N. voting alignments for nations at peace have the same correlation with their interactions as they do for nations in overt conflict."

The remainder of the works relevant to this proposition

present diverse findings that relate one type of foreign policy act with another. Rummel (1969: 238), in the study just mentioned, disconfirms the proposition, finding no relationship between magnitude of dyadic conflict and U.N. voting agreement. Gareau (1970: 966) also studies the U.N., analyzing 330 "cold war" votes in plenary and committee sessions between 1947 and 1967. He reports a "general tendency of states that support the U.S. in the cold war to support as well rightest regimes, Israel over the Arabs, colonialism, and ONUC;" conversely, "pro-communist states tend to be pro-leftist, anti-colonial, pro-Arab, and anti-ONUC."

McGowan (1968: 290) finds that, of 32 African states between 1963 and 1966, if a nation was a high interactor, it received military aid from the Soviet Union; whereas if it was a low interactor, its aid came from NATO members. Also, if a state had a high degree of interaction with the communist system, then it tended to have a high degree of interaction with all states.

The "spillover" effect of one act on others has been studied by several scholars. In a comparison of India and Pakistan, Ray (1966: 61) finds that antagonism towards India affects Pakistan's other foreign relations, but there is no such spillover of India's hostility toward Pakistan. Wolfers' analysis (1940: 383) of the interwar period shows that the British-French conflict over Germany's power and position spilled over to their views on the role of the League of Nations, causing controversy in that area. Young's study (1968: 71) of the 1967 Middle East crisis does not find this relationship: "the pressures to coordinate on global strategic issues do not necessarily 'spill over' to produce increased coordination on a great many specific or local issues." Smoker (1965: 172) is also disconfirming. In a longitudinal analysis of seven nations in the period 1948-1962, he concludes that "a nation may be neutral with or without disarming, or it may disarm with or without being neutral."

Finally, Jensen (1963: 532) studies the effect of conciliatory acts on the overall course of a nation's negotiating behavior. In research on U.S.-U.S.S.R. disarmament, he finds that the level of agreement in these negotiations with respect to reduction levels, staging, inspection, and enforcement has been increasing from 1946 to 1960, indicating that concessions tend to have a cumulative effect on bargaining behavior.

PROPOSITION 115: *The failure of a foreign policy leads to radical, rather than incremental, shifts in that policy.*

Continuing our consideration of the feedback of acts on foreign policy, we formulate this proposition to account for the impact of the success or failure of an act on later decision-making. In research on eight major wars between 1618 and 1918, Klingberg (1966: 167) finds that after a decision to make a final great effort in war has failed, then nations shift their policies rapidly and radically, and the war soon ends. In research on the alliances of Iceland, Thailand, and Australia with the United States between 1949 and 1954, Nuechterlein (1969: 622) finds that if a previous policy of neutrality has failed, then a nation will move to the opposite position when faced with a security threat and form an alliance with a great power.

PROPOSITION 116: *A rise in defense expenditures is positively related to disintegration, tension, and insecurity in the international system.*

With this proposition we move to the second feedback loop—the impact of foreign policy behavior on the politics of the international system. Smoker's studies on defense expenditures present mixed findings on the proposition. In a study (1968: 497) of the arms races before both world wars and during the Cold War, he finds negative feedback between defense expenditure data and international integration as measured by number of NGOs formed per year. But then in a study (1967: 67-68) of the arms races before both world wars between 1948 and 1962, he finds that "a rise in defense expenditure does not necessarily imply an increase in tension in the whole system." Wright's research (1964: 130) confirms the proposition with the finding that rearmament and disarmament have been an important factor in the stability of the balance of power.

PROPOSITION 117: *Conflicts between nations affect the operation of international organizations in which they are members.*

Stoessinger's research (1970: 174-186) on nine cases of Soviet-American interaction in the U.N. since World War II supports this proposition. Conflicts between the two, stemming from attempts to use the U.N. to further "national interests," have been a major influence on the constitutional evolution of the Security Council, the General Assembly, and the Secretariat, and have kept the locus of power shifting among the three branches. The success of the U.N.'s economic projects is dependent on "a minimum of preexistent political harmony or sympathy between the superpowers' national interests." The desire of the U.S. and the U.S.S.R. to further their interests but avoid direct conflict led to the peacekeeping operations of UNEF and ONUC; consensus of the two was necessary to launch these operations, but the exclusion of their direct participation was necessary to sustain them.

Stoessinger's work is supported by Young's analysis (1968: 173) of the 1967 Arab-Isareli war. He finds that "the postures of the great powers, and especially the superpowers, operate as critical determinants of the ability of the United Nations to acquire significant political influence in such cases [of localized crisis]."

A related study is Rubinstein's (1964: 50-51) analysis of U.S. and U.S.S.R. policies toward international economic organizations since World War II. He shows that the competitive global struggle between the two has led to similarities in their behavior: both are opposed to expansion of the operational scope of these organizations, both are concerned with winning parliamentary victories, and both oppose any expansion of fundraising or executive authority in organizations which they believe they could not dominate.

The history of international organizations has been integrally tied to the occurrence of wars. Growth patterns of defensive alliances, IGOs, and NGOs between 1895 and 1964 have all been disrupted by wars; of these three, IGO formation is most affected by war (Pelowski, 1971: 284). As war approaches, membership patterns will be affected. IGO partners "will experience a mild decline in shared memberships if destined to fight alongside each other in the subsequent five to ten years, and a sharp decline if they are to become enemies" (Singer, 1972: 266). After a war, this changes; former allies show a mild postwar decline in shared memberships, whereas former enemies show a clear increase (Singer, 1972: 266). Also after a war, statesmen seem to act on the premise that the creation or continuation of intergovernmental organizations will reduce the incidence of future war. This is the conclusion that Singer and Wallace (1970: 536) draw on the basis of their finding that the number of wars which ended in a half-decade between 1816 and 1945 is positively related to the creation and continuation of IGOs in the following decade.

PROPOSITION 118: *The nature of the power available to nations affects the nature of the international system.*

Based on an analysis of four European state-systems between 1494 and 1945, Dehio (1963: 271) concludes that after each of the great world crises in the past four centuries, sea power emerged as a potent force and made possible the organization, with insular leadership, of conditions to preserve the existing system. Wright (1964: 146) finds that "one factor tending to reduce the frequency of war has been the probability that a war will result in mutual destruction unacceptable to either side." Also, the invention of a new weapon or military formation facilitating aggression is related to the collapse of the balance of power (Wright, 1964: 126).

Miscellaneous Findings

Young's study of the Middle East (1968: 70) includes the finding:

While tacit coordination between the Soviet Union and the United States on several important issues was a critical determinant of the outcome of the 1956 crisis, Soviet-American disagreements became a major source of the failure of third parties to acquire effective influence in 1967.

Wright's research includes several findings relevant to the feedback process. One is that neutrality and the localization of war have been important factors in the restoration of the balance of power (1964: 130). Another is that the collapse of the balance can result from the activities of a conqueror trying to establish tyrannical rule or from the emergence of a new religion or ideology whose enthusiastic adherents try to spread their ideas to other societies (1964: 126). A third finding is that the intervention of powerful states on the periphery of the balance of power system can lead to the collapse of the balance (1964: 126).

Kalela's study (1967: 168) of 1470 roll call votes in the U.N. between 1956 and 1966 reports that the voting cohesion among the Nordic countries is highly dependent on Finland's voting.

There are two studies which relate a nation's foreign policy acts to its national security. Pincus (1965: 188), in an analysis of developed and underdeveloped nations in the 1950s and 1960s, finds that "there is no clearly demonstrable relation between Western economic aid and Western security, broadly defined." Chadwick (1969: 200), in his work on 64 nations in 1955, finds that large force capability is negatively related to natural security.

The foreign policies of the African states which have joined the International Labor Organization, the International Telegraph Union, and the World Health Organization have forced these organizations to reconsider their roles and missions. They have come to focus more on African problems and to change their modes of operation to be more compatible with conditions in Africa (Jacobsen, 1970: 87-88).

Finally, Dowty (1971: 434) finds that as a nation's foreign conflict becomes more severe—as war breaks out or as conflict transcends specific disputes to become general tensions—there is no increase in foreign-linked factionalism, except in Latin America where many of the disputes are minor border clashes.

Evaluation

When we consider that there are three types of propositions in this section—showing the effect of the actor's foreign policy on its domestic politics, on its other foreign policies, and on the international system—then we can realize how little comparative research has actually been done. This is surprising, since the purpose of foreign policy is to bring about some consequence. In other words, why study foreign policy if you are going to ignore the outcomes which decision-makers hope to bring about with that policy? The answer to this question may be found in the focus of the behavioral "revolution." Behavioralism has been oriented toward developing causal theories of behavior, so scholars were satisfied with models and research that "explained" a behavioral output in terms of a number of independent variables. It is only recently, with a renewed interest in public policy, that scholars have begun to examine the consequences of that behavioral output. The result is the preliminary research on the different types of feedback that is surveyed in this last chapter.

Chapter XVI

THE STATE OF THE FIELD

We have now completed our review of the results of over 200 research studies and their many hundreds of separate findings. We have been able to integrate most of these findings under 118 different propositions grouped around the thirteen variable categories of our framework for the comparative analysis of foreign policy. We believe our *Survey* gives an accurate picture of the status of systematic studies of foreign policy as of mid-1972, although we would not claim to have included every relevant study that has ever been published. Indeed, we expect that our readers will quickly point out to us studies that we have missed. Nevertheless, our *Survey* is extensive enough to permit us to ask some basic questions about the state of the field and to offer a few tentative suggestions as to where we think it should move during the rest of this decade.

The most fundamental question is: why do we not have any

theories of foreign policy? This absence of deductively organized theory in our field has serious consequences. Without theory we cannot explain the relationships we "discover" and we can only make predictions of the crudest sort based upon projections from empirical trends, not upon a profound understanding of foreign policy behavior. Without theory to guide our research we must depend on luck and educated guesses to come up with worthwhile research hypotheses. Without theory research becomes ad hoc in the extreme, with no justification provided for the selection of cases, with no system to the definition and measurement of concepts, and with no consistency in the use of research techniques and data-processing routines. In brief, a field without theory is hardly an area of disciplined scientific inquiry. Since the comparative study of foreign policy lacks both middle-range and general theories of foreign policy behavior it fails to meet the basic objective of any science: a body of theoretically organized knowledge that is based on cumulative empirical research.

A simple-minded answer to our question is that it is not possible to make theories of complex political behavior like foreign policy. In our view, the relative success that economists have achieved in developing deductive theories of selected aspects of economic behavior suggests that rigorous theorizing about complex human behavior is not, in principle, impossible. Recent advances in the theory of voting bodies and coalition theory also demonstrate that this type of theory is not beyond political scientists.

A basic reason for the lack of systematic foreign policy theory of the type discussed in Chapter I is that an unfortunate division of labor has developed in our field which tends to separate the "theorists" from the "empirical researchers." A glance at our bibliography will demonstrate that many of the most prominent names in the field of foreign policy "theory" have not authored empirical comparative studies—the only type of research capable of validating theory. On the other hand, most of the authors of the studies we have surveyed have not tried their hands at broad-range theoretical essays. If the comparative study of foreign policy is to develop as a field in the social sciences, then a new generation of students must appear who will be both theorists and researchers, for this present "division of labor" is both unnecessary and harmful.

New modes of theorizing must be tried if the field is to advance. At present, general theory tends not to be open to systematic study because it is either too vague to be tested or not even designed to be tested, since it is prescription masquerading as explanatory theory. Recognizably empirical theory is so limited in what it purports to explain and predict that it is uninteresting except to a few specialists. In our view, scholars who are theoretically oriented researchers need to devote more attention to formal theory as embodied in mathematical models and computer simulations. Selected aspects of foreign policy behavior may be open to analysis via deductive theory, as done in economics or by Riker in the area of political coalitions.[1] Such theories will probably be quite narrow in terms of the range of behavior they account for, but they could nevertheless be quite useful in what we might call the "micro-theory" of foreign policy decision-making behavior. Certain convergencies are now appearing in the area of economic exchange theory and psychological and small group learning-exchange theory that could be a rewarding source for scholars with a deductive orientation.

In the area of what we might call the "macro-theory" of foreign policy behavior by organizations and national societies, the application of computer simulations to the analysis of the complex, multi-level, nonlinear, and mutually interdependent reality that we study seems appropriate. Brunner and Brewer have recently presented an all-computer simulation model of political development which deserves close study by students of foreign policy phenomena.[2] Of course, simulations can be applied to micro-problems and deductive theory can be applied to macro-problems. Since both approaches demand the explicit statement of theoretical relationships in the form of systems of equations, cross-level linkages may prove possible to state.

Further evidence of the prescientific status of the comparative study of foreign policy is the idiographic nature of much of the research surveyed. All of the comparative case studies in our *Survey* and many of the more statistical works employ spatio-temporal terms (names of countries and individuals, specific time periods, and so on) that limit the scope of any generalizations that can be derived from the research. The goal of comparative research is to substitute variables like "level of modernization" for spatio-temporal terms like "China" and "France."[3]

That is, as part of the social sciences the comparative study of foreign policy seeks to state general explanatory sentences. To be general, a sentence must not state or imply proper names. To be explanatory, a sentence must relate two or more variables. For example,

(1) France is a nonconforming alliance member

is not a general sentence, because it contains a proper name. In a similar fashion,

(2) There are alliances

or

(3) Foreign policy decision-makers seek to maximize the power of their countries

are general sentences, but they are not explanatory for they do not relate variables. Sentence (2) merely states a fact about a finite class of things called "alliances"—that it is not an empty set. Sentence (3) is perhaps less clear, but if we restate it as

(3^1) In every country that Morgenthau has studied, he found that decision-makers tried to increase the power of their country

we see that it is not a sentence that relates two or more variables. Sentences (3) and (3^1) are empirical generalizations at the very best. However, if we say

(4) There is a negative relationship between a nation's political development and its support for international law and organizations (Proposition 20)

we have a general explanatory sentence. This is made even clearer if we restate (4) as

(4^1) For every nation, if it is politically developed, then it will not support international law and organizations.

No proper names are stated or implied by sentences (4) and (4^1), so they are general; and they both relate the variables of political development and supportive foreign policy behavior, so they are explanatory.[4]

Now, while most of the propositions in this *Survey* are stated in this general explanatory form, most of the findings upon which they are based are not so stated. Foreign policy research must become more comparative and, in line with notions of Przeworski and Teune, attempt to create nomothetic explanatory sentences by making variables out of the country and area-specific findings so far developed.

Thus, our second question is: Why has the study of foreign policy remained so idiographic? Our answer is two-fold. First, qualitatively oriented scholars have continued to do case studies rather than comparisons of two or more cases. One does not have to use numbers to generate scientifically useful findings, but one has to be comparative to make such findings. Many excellent scholars have failed to appreciate this and they continue to do single country case studies, although it is easy to demonstrate the scientific uselessness of such research. Suppose that the researcher's "hypothesis" or "problem" is that he thinks U causes V. He then proceeds to examine in great detail some case and, in fact, he does find U with V. However, he finds W, X, Y, and Z present as well. Thus,

a. hypothesis: U and V
b. finding: U, V, W, X, Y, and Z.

If such were the case—and it always is, for two variables never exist in isolation from other factors—the scholar could not

assert that U causes V, for the alternative hypotheses that V
is caused by X or W or Y or Z or some combination of them
is also consistent with the evidence. Only in an instance
where the scholar found the following:

a. hypothesis:	U and V
b. finding, case 1:	U and V, W, X, Y, Z.
case 2:	S, T, U and V.

or something similar could he assert that U causes V, for U
alone is always present when V is present.[5] Therefore, as
long as many of our most competent scholars continue to do
case studies, foreign policy studies will remain idiographic.

The second reason for the continuing idiographic bias in
the field is that quantitatively oriented scholars have tended
to collect data prior to theorizing and then they have
proceeded to analyze these data in a bivariate fashion. In the
end, we must recognize that a theoretical justification is the
only acceptable reason to collect a given set of data or to
apply a particular technique to the analysis of the data
collected. Much of the most technically sophisticated work in
comparative foreign policy studies has been theoretical ex
post facto. When this happens, place names and time periods
are introduced to make sense out of the "significant" but
unexpected "findings." This is particularly noticeable in
studies of U.N. voting behavior.

The favorite analytical technique in foreign policy studies
of a statistical type has been bivariate correlation, which
leaves a great deal to be desired. Regression analysis and its
related techniques, such as path analysis and simultaneous-
equation estimation techniques, are the more appropriate
multivariate statistical routines to apply to quantified foreign
policy data because they force the analyst to think of controls
and in cause-and-effect terms (independent-dependent variables, exogenous-endogenous variables), even if empirical
analyses can never prove causation.

In light of these remarks, it goes without saying that
further research is needed on all of the independent variable

clusters in this *Survey's* framework and on all types of foreign policy behavior. Much greater emphasis must be placed on replication so that, as each finding is confirmed, it can be related to and used to support or modify a theoretical proposition. Only through this painstaking process can we build a body of cumulative knowledge in foreign policy studies. Yet, as our *Survey* has demonstrated time and again, most research in comparative foreign policy is original and unreplicated.

Our third question, therefore, is: why are there not more replications in foreign policy studies? A very simple reason is that most of the research surveyed in this book is just not replicable. Researchers usually fail to be specific and detailed enough in the writing of their research reports to permit someone else to replicate their work. While this could be intentional in order to prevent others from encroaching on carefully tended academic gardens, we prefer to think that it is largely unintentional and a consequence of the prescientific attitudes of the profession. For, even in the relatively few instances where a study is replicable, it has rarely been replicated. As Karl Deutsch has commented:

We suffer from the curse of enforced originality which makes it a crime for a graduate student to replicate somebody else's experiment and forces the unhappy man to think up a new wrinkle on every experiment. I wish we could get an inter-university agreement that we expect everybody who earns a degree to do two things: first, to replicate honestly one experiment in social science and then, if he must, invent a new one. If physicists and chemists had not replicated each other's experiments, they would still be in the age of alchemy.[6]

As authors of a study which has made us painfully aware of the lack of replications in foreign policy research, we heartily endorse Deutsch's recommendation.

If we are to replicate each other's research, then our data sets must be made more readily available to each other. Some specialists in international relations research and the comparative study of foreign policy have taken this obligation to the profession at large seriously and they have made their data readily available to other scholars: the WEIS project, the DON project, and the Correlates of War project are notable examples. For, in Deutsch's words again,

So long as data are thought of as reposing in archives, and the custodians of these archives think of themselves as librarians—and if possible as librarians of rare medieval books which can only be let out with infinite caution—we will not have much in the way of social science. As we make social science data as freely reproducible and as readily available as elementary chemicals are available to chemists, as we get the social science data into the laboratories, and as our data archives and repositories become linked with data laboratories, we shall witness, I believe, a renaissance of social science. [7]

We are clearly not yet at this golden age of social science that Deutsch envisages, but we must all try to meet his demand for more readily available data before we can deny the correctness of his prediction. Thus, a fourth question we would ask of ourselves and our readers is: have you made your data available to other centers of research on comparative foreign policy?

In spite of the statement that research is needed in all aspects of the field, it will be useful to point out those areas which have been particularly neglected. Except for the work of the Stanford group on the pre-World War I crisis, there are few comparative studies of individual variables. It would be interesting to relate the research of psychologists on motivation to foreign policy outputs. Elite variables and establishment variables have largely been ignored; the influence of the foreign affairs and the military bureaucracies is a particularly intriguing question for comparative studies. Indeed, the whole subject of influence groups, an almost universal phenomenon, has hardly been investigated on a comparative basis. Among the large number of works that focus on political variables, only a few studies consider the role of parties or various pressure groups in foreign policy-making. Another conspicuous variable missing from Chapter VI is civil war. In light of the recent conflicts in Pakistan, Nigeria,

Ceylon, and Ireland, the impact of civil war is a highly relevant question. Governmental variables have received a good deal of attention; but scholars have omitted consideration of the influence of executive-legislative relations and the size of, and changes in, the national budget. Most of the societal variables except population size and most cultural variables have been neglected.

A relatively large amount of work has been done on the other's policies and systemic variable clusters; but it is very diverse, so that any specific variable might be used in only one study. Much replication is needed.

An important aspect of comparative research on foreign policy behavior that has been grossly neglected is highlighted by the framework we have used throughout this *Survey*, It is the levels of analysis problem, which relates to inferences across levels that in our framework range from the individual decision-maker to the entire international system. Many of the studies surveyed by us come close to committing what is known as the ecological fallacy—making inferences about relationships at the level of individuals from data gathered on aggregate units like nations. Thus, conflict acts received by a state are found to be positively related to conflict behavior emitted by the state. It would be an instance of the ecological fallacy to say that such a relationship observed at the level of the nation-state is evidence in support of the hypothesis that "when decision-makers are threatened, they respond by acting threateningly themselves," for the latter is a statement about the behavior of individuals. In a similar fashion, the *individualistic fallacy* ascribes relationships found to be true at the level of individuals to relationships among variable characteristics of groups, like nation-states. It is not necessarily true that, if an individual is frustrated and he responds aggressively, a national foreign policy when blocked will cause the state to react in an aggressive fashion. A number of different types of inferential fallacies have been identified. Students of the comparative study of foreign policy who must deal with individuals and organizations up to and including the international system are particularly prone to make them.[8]

The problem of fallacious inference across different levels is an aspect of the larger problem of the analysis of parts and wholes. The only published analysis of this problem in the field of foreign policy studies is insightful, but not systematic.[9] If the comparative study of foreign policy is to progress, intensive analysis is needed of the conditions under which characteristics of a foreign policy elite, for example, may be used to explain the behavior of nation-states or how aspects of the international system (the whole) can be used to predict the behavior of its member-states (the parts).

Turning to the dependent variable, we can say that most types of foreign policy output have been considered. However, one notices that conflict behavior has been a much more frequent object of study than has cooperative behavior. This is probably the result of the Cold War atmosphere, but both scholars and policy-makers have begun to realize that cooperation is at least as important a type of behavior as conflict. In addition, there is a need for research on national activity in organizations other than the U.N. (specifically functional agencies and regional organizations), on limited regional wars, on subversive intervention, on penetration, on negotiations, on the use (and abuse) of international law, and on specific policy issue-areas.

A problem of particular importance in this regard is the absence of a widely accepted typology of foreign policy behavior. Most scholars measure foreign policy in highly idiosyncratic fashions. Their research findings are not comparable or cumulative because they conceptualize and operationalize foreign policy differently. Empirically grounded typologies of foreign policy such as Kegley's (1971) recent dissertation deserve a particular emphasis at this time.

A great deal of further research is necessary on the influence of decision-making variables and on the two feedback processes. Research in these two important areas of our field is very sketchy, and scholars have a good opportunity to start from the ground and build a body of research that is solidly based on theory, if they can state it.

On a more general level, we strongly recommend that scholars turn to the task of establishing the relative potencies of independent variables. No theory can be generated from the framework and propositions presented in this inventory until we know which variables are more important determinants of foreign policy behavior in which issue-areas and for which types of states. Efforts to develop this type of "pre-theory" can use the works of Rosenau (1968) and Moore (1970) as models. Simple bivariate analysis may be necessary in the early stages of the development of a discipline, but it can only get us so far; eventually scholars will have to determine what variables are the key factors in different kinds of situations.

This raises a final question of considerable significance: why would anyone want to determine what variables are the key factors in different kinds of situations? One answer, which is legitimate, is that one simply wants to understand the way the world works. This is the scientist's answer. But the scientist is a citizen and usually a husband or wife, mother or father, as well as professional scholar. Indeed, most of us study the foreign policy behavior of nation-states because we find it dramatic, gratifying, or fearsome, as well as puzzling and in need of systematic analysis. Many specialists seek, via their expertise, to become part of the policy-making process as advisors and temporary diplomats. Foreign policy is public policy, and—at least with respect to the policies of our own country (whichever that might be)—we feel obligated to criticize and to support it as well as to study it. Thus, an essential aspect of the comparative study of foreign policy is the *evaluation* of past policy from a normative point of view (was it good or bad as measured against some set of values) and the *prescription* of future policy (will it promote or hinder the achievement of values we hold?).

There is no necessary reason why evaluative and prescriptive studies must be nonsystematic; but most are, for we have not found in our *Survey* of systematic studies many that were undertaken with a stated normative goal. In our view, this is an unfortunate state of affairs. If normative preferences are not explicitly stated, then they are always implicit in the research—for even the desire to do a "scientific" study is a normative decision. In addition, scholarship is a social process which in the end must justify its cost to society by the benefits it creates. Many social scientists feel today that social science is a tool in the struggle for a better world—for example, a world with a more equitable distribution of wealth and less violence. If this is the type of world one would like to shape, then one must determine the variables that affect violence and income differentials between countries. For many, then, their systematic orientation to the study of foreign policy derives from their normative interests in policy evaluation and prescription. Such a position is legitimate too, and peace research has produced many of the studies included in our *Survey*.

The comparative study of foreign policy behavior is still a young field, but we have made considerable progress. We have learned something about the causes and consequences of foreign policy behavior, although with varying degrees of confidence in our knowledge. But more basically, we have learned that a complex social phenomenon can be accounted for by a number of types of independent variables. We have learned that concepts comprising both independent and dependent variables can be operationalized and validly measured, and that analysis using these measures can lead to generalizations applicable across different political systems. We have learned, in other words, that the comparative study of foreign policy is an emerging field in the social sciences. The propositions synthesized from research in this *Survey* are the foundation of that science. It is the present task of social scientists to build upon that foundation.

NOTES

1. For example, Anthony Downs, *An Economic Theory of Democracy* (New York: Harper & Row, 1957); and William Riker, *The Theory of Political Coalitions* (New Haven: Yale University Press, 1962).

2. Ronald D. Brunner and Garry D. Brewer, *Organized Complexity: Empirical Theories of Political Development* (New York: Free Press, 1971).

3. Adam Przeworski and Henry Teune, *The Logic of Comparative Social Inquiry* (New York: Wiley-Interscience, 1970), pp. 5-11, 24-30.

4. Morris Zelditch, Jr., "Intelligible Comparisons," pp. 267-307 in I. Vallier (ed.) *Comparative Methods in Sociology* (Berkeley: University of California Press, 1971.

5. *Ibid.*

6. Karl W. Deutsch, "Recent Trends in Research Methods in Political Science," in J. S. Charlesworth (ed.) *A Design for Political Science* (Philadelphia: American Academy of Political and Social Science Monograph 6, 1966), p. 42.

7. *Ibid.*, p. 55.

8. Hayward R. Alker, Jr., "A Typology of Ecological Fallacies," in M. Dogan and S. Rokkan (eds.) *Quantitative Ecological Analysis* (Cambridge: MIT Press, 1969); and Michael T. Hannan, *Problems of Aggregation and Disaggregation in Sociological Research* (Chapel Hill: University of North Carolina Institute for Research in Social Science, 1970).

9. David Singer, "The Level-of-Analysis Problem in International Relations," pp. 77-92 in K. Knorr and S. Verba, *The International System* (Princeton, N.J.: Princeton University Press, 1961.

REFERENCES

This bibliography serves two functions. First, it represents a traditional bibliography, listing in alphabetical order by author every comparative study cited in the text. After each bibliographical listing, in brackets, we give the pages where the work is referred to in the book. The bibliography thus comprises both an article and author index. We hope it will be more useful than the usual bibliography provided in volumes of this sort. A traditional subject index follows at the end of the book.

ABEL, T. (1941) "The element of decision in the pattern of war." Amer. Soc. Rev. 6: 853-859. [191]

ALGER, C. F. (1968) "Interaction in a committee of the United Nations General Assembly," pp. 51-84 in J. D. Singer (ed.) Quantitative International Politics. New York: Free Press. [114, 123, 205]

——— and S. J. BRAMS (1967) "Patterns of representation in national capitals and intergovernmental organizations." World Politics 19 (July): 646-657. [115, 139, 140]

ALKER, H. R., Jr. (1969) "Supranationalism in the United Nations," pp. 697-710 in J. N. Rosenau (ed.) International Politics and Foreign Policy. New York: Free Press. [100, 167]

——— (1964) "Dimensions of conflict in the General Assembly." Amer. Pol. Sci. Rev. 56 (March): 642-657. [100, 111, 121, 130, 137, 167]

——— and D. J. PUCHALA (1968) "Trends in economic partnership: the North Atlantic area, 1928-1963," pp. 287-316 in J. D. Singer (ed.) Quantitative International Politics. New York: Free Press. [143, 178]

——— and B. R. RUSSETT (1965) World Politics in the General Assembly. New Haven: Yale Univ. Press. [84, 100, 111, 121, 136-137, 167-168]

ALMOND, G. A. (1968) "Public opinion and the development of space technology: 1957-60," pp. 86-110 in R. L. Merritt and D. J. Puchala (eds.) Western European Perspectives on International Affairs. New York: Praeger. [153-154]

ANDREAS, C. R. (1969) "To receive from kings: an examination of government-to-government aid and its unintended conseqeunces." J. of Social Issues 25, 1: 167-180. [61, 154]

AROSALO, U. (1970) "A model of international interaction in Western Europe." J. of Peace Research 7: 247-258. [85, 170]

BANDYOPADHAYA, J. (1968) "Making of foreign policy: a tentative subsystemic model for South Asia." South Asian Studies 3 (July): 27-39. [107-108, 125]

BANKS, A. S. and P. M. GREGG (1971) "Grouping political systems: Q-factor analysis of A Cross-Polity Survey," pp. 311-320 in J. V. Gillespie and B. A. Nesvold (eds.) Macro-Quantitative Analysis. Beverly Hills: Sage Publications.

BENJAMIN, R. W. and L. J. EDINGER (1971) "Conditions for military control over foreign policy decisions in major states: an historical explanation." J. of Conflict Resolution 15: 5-31. [61, 69-70, 76, 94, 97, 108, 192]

BONHAM, G. M. (1970) "Participation in regional assemblies: effects on attitudes of Scandanavian parliamentarians." J. of Common Market Studies 8: 325-326. [66]

BRAMS, S. J. (1969) "The structure of influence relationships in the international system," pp. 583-599 in J. N. Rosenau (ed) International Politics and Foreign Policy. New York: Free Press. [142, 158]

——— (1966) "Transaction flows in the international system." Amer. Pol. Sci. Rev. 60: 880-898. [102, 139, 140, 171-172].

BRZEZINSKI, Z. and S. P. HUNTINGTON (1963) Political Power: USA/USSR. New York: Viking. [71, 72, 86-87, 126, 135, 150]

BUNKER, R. (1969) "Linkages and the foreign policy of Peru: 1958-1966." Western Pol. Q. 22: 280-297. [77, 108, 155]

BURGESS, P. M. (1968) Elite Images and Foreign Policy Outcomes: A Study of Norway. Columbus: Ohio State Univ. Press. [53-54, 162-163]

CAMPBELL, J. T. and L. S. CAIN (1965) "Public opinion and the outbreak of war." J. of Conflict Resolution 9: 318-329. [120-121]

CATTELL, R. B. (1949) "The dimensions of culture patterns by factorization of national characters." J. of Abnormal and Social Psychology 44: 443-469. [122-123, 128-129, 130]

CHADWICK, R. W. (1969) "An inductive empirical analysis of intra- and international behavior aimed at a partial extension of inter-nation simulation theory." J. of Peace Research 6: 193-214. [96, 102, 115, 196, 210]

CHALMERS, D. A. (1969) "Developing on the periphery: external factors in Latin American politics," pp. 67-93 in J. N. Rosenau (ed.) Linkage Politics. New York: Free Press. [155, 197]

CHOUCRI, N. (1969a) "The nonalignment of Afro-Asian states: policy perception and behavior." Canadian J. of Pol. Sci. 2: 1-17. [54, 182]

––– (1969b) "The perceptual base of non-alignment." J. of Conflict Resolution 13: 57-74. [182]

––– and R. C. NORTH (1969) "The determinants of international violence." Peace Research Society Papers 12: 33-63. [96, 109, 118-119, 141, 166]

CLARK, J. F., M. K. O'LEARY, and E. R. WITTKOPF (1971) "National attributes associated with dimensions of support for the United Nations." Internatl. Organization 25, 1: 1-25. [100, 112-113, 122; 138, 152]

CLEMENS, W. C., Jr. (1966) "Underlying factors in soviet arms control policy: problems of systematic analysis." Peace Research Society Papers 6: 51-70. [77, 103, 108]

COBB, R. W. and C. ELDER (1970) International Community: A regional and Global Study. New York: Holt, Rinehart & Winston. [86, 130, 138, 139, 171, 172, 173]

COHEN, B. C. (1969) "National-international linkages: superpolities," pp. 125-146 in J. N. Rosenau (ed.) Linkage Politics. New York: Free Press. [162, 196]

COLLINS, J. N. (1967) "Foreign conflict behavior and domestic disorder in Africa." Ph.D. dissertation. Evanston, Ill.: Northwestern University. [80]

CRAIG, G. A. (1961) "Totalitarian approaches to diplomatic negotiations," pp. 107-125 in A. O. Sarkissian (ed.) Studies in Diplomatic History and Historiography. London: Longmans, Green. [72]

DEHIO, L. (1963) The Precarious Balance: The Politics of Power in Europe, 1494-1945. London: Chatto and Windus: [149, 209]

DEUTSCH, K. W. (1960a) "The propensity to international transactions." Pol. Studies 8: 147-155. [122]

––– (1960b) "Toward an inventory of basic trends and patterns in comparative and international politics." Amer. Pol. Sci. Rev. 54: 34-57. [115, 130, 138-139, 140, 172]

––– C. I. BLISS, and A. ECKSTEIN (1962) "Population, sovereignty and the shape of foreign trade." Econ. Development & Cultural Change 10: 353-366. [114, 122, 139]

––– and A. ECKSTEIN (1961) "National industrialization and the declining share of the international economic sector, 1890-1959." World Politics 13: 267-299. [114, 122]

––– and R. L. MERRITT (1965) "Effects of events on national and international images," pp. 132-187 in H. C. Kelman (ed.) International Behavior. New York: Holt, Rinehart & Winston. [200]

DOWTY, A. (1971) "Foreign-linked factionalism as a historical pattern." J. of Conflict Resolution 15: 429-442. [131, 177, 211]

EAST, M. A. (1972) "Status discrepancy and violence in the international system: an empirical analysis," pp. 299-316 in J. N. Rosenau, V. Davis, and M. A. East (eds.) The Analysis of International Politics. New York: Free Press. [165]

––– (1969) "Rank-dependent interaction and mobility: two aspects of international stratification." Peace Research Society Papers 14: 113-127. [102, 170]

––– and P. M. GREGG (1967) "Factors influencing cooperation and conflict in the international system." Internat. Studies Q. 11: 244-269. [76, 79, 89, 99, 109, 120, 162, 205]

ECKHARDT, W. and R. K. WHITE (1967) "A test of the mirror-image hypothesis: Kennedy and Krushchev." J. of Conflict Resolution 11: 325-332. [184]

ELLIS, W. W. and J. SALZBERG (1965) "Africa and the U.N.: a statistical note." Amer. Behav. Scientist 8, 8: 30-32. [100, 111, 121, 136, 152]

ETZIONI, A. (1967) "The Kennedy experiment." Western Pol. Q. 20: pages 361-380. [150]

FEIERABEND, I. and R. FEIERABEND (1969) "Level of development and internation behavior," pp. 135-188 in R. Butwell (ed.) Foreign Policy and the Developing Nation. Lexington: Univ. of Kentucky Press. [80, 81, 96, 109, 110, 114, 118, 128, 134-135, 149]

FINLAY, D. J., O. R. HOLSTI, and R. R. FAGEN (1967) Enemies in Politics. Chicago: Rand McNally. [104, 127, 202]

FOX, A. B. (1959) The Power of Small States: Diplomacy in World War II. Chicago: Univ. of Chicago Press. [87, 103, 110, 148, 158, 174-175]

GALTUNG, J. (1966) "East-West interaction patterns." J. of Peace Research 3: 146-176. [169, 170, 177]

GAMSON, W. A. and A. MODIGLIANI (1965) "Soviet responses to Western foreign policy 1946-1953." Peace Research Society Papers 3: 47-78. [150]

GAREAU, F. H. (1970) "Cold-war cleavages as seen from the United Nations General Assembly: 1947-1967." J. of Politics 32: 929-168. [136, 206]

GEORGE, A. L., D. K. HALL, and W. E. SIMONS (1971) The Limits of Coercive Diplomacy: Laos-Cuba-Vietnam. Boston: Little, Brown. [72-73, 78, 102-103, 151-152, 189]

GORDON, M. R. (1969) Conflict and Consensus in Labour's Foreign Policy: 1914-1965. Stanford: Stanford Univ. Press. [89]

GREGG, P. M. and A. S. BANKS (1965) "Dimensions of political systems: factor analysis of *A Cross-Polity Survey*." Amer. Pol. Sci. Rev. 59: 602-614. [70, 80-81, 94]

GREGG, R. W. (1965) "The Latin American bloc in United Nations elections." Southwestern Social Sci. Q. 46: 146-154. [101, 112]

HAAS, E. B. (1968) The Uniting of Europe: Political, Social, and Economic Forces, 1950-1957. Stanford: Stanford Univ. Press. [88, 152, 175-176]

HAAS, M. (1969a) "Communication factors in decision-making." Peace Research Society Papers 12: 65-86. [57, 77, 127, 187, 191]

――― (1969b) "Toward the study of biopolitics: cross-sectional analysis of mortality rates." Behav. Sci. 14: 257-280. [78-79, 201-202]

――― (1968a) "Social change and national aggressiveness, 1900-1960," pp. 215-244 in J. D. Singer (ed.) Quantitative International Politics. New York: Free Press. [120]

――― (1968b) "Societal asymmetries and world peace." Proceedings of the Internatl. Peace Research Assn. Conference 2: 70-110. [98-99, 166]

――― (1965) "Societal approaches to the study of war." J. of Peace Research 2: 307-324. [80, 109, 120]

HANRIEDER, W. H. (1967) West German Foreign Policy, 1949-1963. Stanford: Stanford Univ. Press. [116, 158, 182-183, 197, 202]

HERO, A. O., Jr. (1969) "American Negroes and U.S. foreign policy: 1937-1967." J. of Conflict Resolution 13: 220-251. [200]

HILSMAN, R. (1967) To Move a Nation: The Politics of Foreign Policy in the Administration of John F. Kennedy. Garden City: Doubleday [70, 77]

HILTON, G. (1971) "A closed and open model analysis of hostility in crisis." J. of Peace Research 8: 249-262. [55, 60]

HOADLEY, J. S. and S. HASEGAWA (1971) "Sino-Japanese relations, 1950-1970: an application of the linkage model of international politics." Internatl. Studies Q. 15: 131-157. [143-144, 171]

HOFFMANN, F. (1967) "The functions of economic sanctions: a comparative analysis." J. of Peace Research 4: 140-159. [78, 202]

HOLSTI, K. J. (1970) "National role conceptions in the study of foreign policy." Internatl. Studies Q. 14: 233-309. [202-203]

HOLSTI, O. R. (1970) "Individual differences in 'definition of the situation.' " J. of Conflict Resolution 14: 233-309. [202-203]

――― (1965) "Perceptions of time, perceptions of alternatives, and patterns of communication as factors in crisis decision-making." Peace Research Society Papers 3: 79-120. [58-59, 60]

――― and R. C. NORTH (1970) "Perceptions of hostility and financial indicies during the 1914 crisis," pp. 112-132 in H. Rosenbaum (ed.),

Readings on the International Political System. Englewood Cliffs, N.J.: Prentice-Hall. [196]

――― (1966) "Comparative data from content analysis: perceptions of hostility and economic variables in the 1914 crisis," pp. 169-190 in R. L. Merritt and S. Rokkan (eds.) Comparing Nations. New Haven: Yale Univ. Press. [196]

――― and (1965) "The history of human conflict," pp. 155-171 in E. B. McNeil (ed.) The Nature of Human Conflict. Englewood Cliffs, N.J.: Prentice Hall. [59, 183]

――― and R. A. BRODY (1969) "Measuring affect and action in international reaction models: empirical materials from the 1962 Cuban crisis," pp. 679-696 in J. N. Rosenau (ed.) International Politics and Foreign Policy. New York: Free Press. [150-151, 187]

――― (1968) "Perception and action in the 1914 crisis," pp. 123-158 in J. D. Singer (ed.) Quantitative International Politics. New York: Free Press. [56-57, 183, 196]

――― and J. D. SULLIVAN (1969) "National-international linkages: France and China as nonconforming alliance members," pp. 147-195 in J. N. Rosenau (ed.) Linkage Politics. New York: Free Press. [87-88, 103, 162, 177, 202]

HOLT, R. T. and J. E. TURNER (1969) "Insular polities," pp. 199-236 in J. N. Rosenau (ed.) Linkage Politics. New York: Free Press. [198]

HOPMANN, P. T. (1967) "International conflict and cohesion in the Communist system." Internatl. Studies Q. 11: 212-236. [170-171]

HOVET, T., Jr. (1963) Africa in the United Nations. Evanston, Ill.: Northwestern Univ. Press. [140, 190, 203]

JACOBSEN, H. K. (1970) "New states and functional international organizations: a preliminary report," pp. 74-97 in R. W. Cox (ed.) The Politics of International Organizations. New York: Praeger. [168, 176, 203, 210-211]

JACOBSEN, K. (1967) "Voting behavior of the Nordic countries in the General Assembly." Cooperation & Conflict 2: 139-157. [190]

JENSEN, L. (1969a) "Levels of political development and interstate conflict in South Asia," pp. 189-209, in R. Butwell (ed.) Foreign Policy and the Developing Nations. Lexington: Univ. of Kentucky Press. [80]

――― (1969b) "Postwar democratic polities: national-international linkages in the defense policy of the defeated states," pp. 304-323 in J. N. Rosenau (ed.) Linkage Politics. New York: Free Press. [76, 162, 174]

――― (1965) "Military capabilities and bargaining behavior." J. of Conflict Resolution 9: 155-163. [102]

――― (1963) "Soviet-American bargaining behavior in postwar disarmament negotiations." J. of Conflict Resolution 7: 522-541. [150, 206-207]

JERVIS, R. (1968) "Hypotheses on misperception." World Politics 20: 454-479. [184, 185-186]

KALELA, J. (1967) "The Nordic group in the General Assembly." Cooperation & Conflict 2: 158-170. [189-190, 210]

KATZ, F. E. and F. V. PIRET (1964) "Circuitous participation in politics." Amer. J. of Sociology 69: 367-373. [201]

KAY, D. A. (1969) "The impact of African states on the United Nations." Internatl. Organization 23: 20-47. [137, 190]

KEGLEY, C. W., Jr. (1971) "Toward the construction of an empirically grounded typology of foreign policy output behavior." Ph.D. dissertation. Syracuse, N.Y.: Syracuse University. [37, 172, 173, 193, 204, 205, 222]

KEIM, W. D. (1971) "Nations and Conflict Individuality." J. of Peace Research 8: 287-292. [96, 97, 142-143]

KLINGBERG, F. L. (1966) "Predicting the termination of war: battle casualties and population losses." J. of Conflict Resolution 10: 129-171. [121, 207]

――― (1952) "The historical alternation of moods in American foreign policy." World Politics 4: 239-273. [185]

LAMBELET, J. C. (1971) "A dynamic model of the arms race in the Middle East, 1953-1965." General Systems Yearbook 16: 145-167. [57-58, 110, 148, 151]

LEGVOLD, R. (1970) Soviet Policy in West Africa. Cambridge: Harvard Univ. Press. [89]

LIDSTROM, J. and C. Wiklund (1967) "The Nordic countries in the General Assembly and its two political committees." Cooperation & Conflict 2: 171-187. [136, 175, 189-190]

LUARD, E. (1967) "Conciliation and deterrence: a comparison of political strategies in the interwar and postwar periods." World Politics 19: 167-189. [177]

MCCLELLAND, C. A. and G. Hoggard (1969) "Conflict patterns in the interactions among nations," pp. 711-724 in J. N. Rosenau (ed.) International Politics and Foreign Policy. New York: Free Press. [37]

McGOWAN, P. J. (1970) "Theoretical approaches to the comparative study of foreign policy." Ph.D. Dissertation. Evanston, Ill.: Northwestern University. [66, 73, 76, 107, 123, 131]

――― (1969) "The patterns of African diplomacy: a quantitative comparison." J. of Asian & African Studies 4: 202-221. [108, 142, 143]

——— (1968) "Africa and non-alignment: a comparative study of foreign policy." Internatl. Studies Q. 12: 262-295. [101-102, 113-114, 122, 158, 206]

McKENNA, J. C. (1962) Diplomatic Protest in Foreign Policy. Chicago: Loyola Univ. Press. [72, 78, 87, 103, 116, 153, 188, 191, 193]

MERRITT, R. L. (1969) "Noncontiguity and political integration," pp. 237-272 in J. N. Rosenau (ed.) Linkage Politics. New York: Free Press. [164]

MIDLARSKY, M. and R. TANTER (1967) "Toward a theory of political instability in Latin America." J. of Peace Research 4: 209-227. [154-155]

MITCHELL, W. C. (1971) "The role of stress in the war in Vietnam: an analysis of United States actions and public statements, 1964-1967." Peace Research Society Papers 17: 47-60. [56, 58, 59, 60, 201]

MODELSKI, G. (1964) "International settlement of internal war," pp. 122-153 in J. N. Rosenau (ed.) International Aspects of Civil Strife. Princeton: Princeton Univ. Press. [196]

MOORE, D. W. (1970) "Governmental and societal influences on foreign policy: a partial examination of Rosenau's adaptation model." Ph.D. dissertation. Columbus: Ohio State University. [94, 108, 117-118, 223]

MUELLER, J. E. (1971) "Trends in popular support for the wars in Korea and Vietnam.'. Amer. Pol. Sci. Rev. 65: 358-375. [201]

——— (1970) "Presidential popularity from Truman to Johnson." Amer. Pol. Sci. Rev. 64: 18-34. [201]

NESS, G. D. (1969) "Foreign policy and social change," pp. 41-66 in R. Butwell (ed.) Foreign Policy and the Developing Nations. Lexington: Univ. of Kentucky Press. [73, 86, 87, 188, 198]

NORTH, R. C. (1967) "Perception and action in the 1914 crisis." J. of Internatl. Affairs 21: 103-122. [56, 192]

——— R. A. BRODY, and O. R. HOLSTI (1964) "Some empirical data on the conflict spiral." Peace Research Society Papers 1: 1-14. [54-55, 56]

——— and N. CHOUCRI (1968) "Background conditions to the outbreak of the First World War." Peace Research Society Papers 9: 125-137. [166]

NEUCHTERLEIN, D. E. (1969) "Small states in alliances: Iceland, Thailand, and Australia." Orbis 13: 600-623. [144, 149, 207]

O'LEARY, M. K. (1969) "Linkages between domestic and international politics in underdeveloped nations," pp. 324-346 in J. N. Rosenau (ed.) Linkage Politics. New York: Free Press. [114, 140]

OTTERBEIN, K. F. (1968) "Cross-cultural studies of armed combat." Buffalo Studies 4, 1: 91-109. [199]

PELOWSKI, A. L. (1971) "On the use of a quasi-experimental design in the study of international organization and war." J. of Peace Research 8: 279-285. [209]

PHILLIPS, W. R. (1971) "The dynamics of behavioral action and reaction in international conflict." Peace Research Society Papers 17: 31-46. [149-150]

PINCUS, J. A. (1965) Economic Aid and International Cost Sharing. Baltimore: Johns Hopkins Press. [112, 114, 156-157, 210]

RAY, J. K. (1966) "India and Pakistan as factors in each other's foreign policies." Internatl. Studies 8: 49-63. [206]

REINTON, P. O. (1967) "International structure and international integration: the case of Latin America." J. of Peace Research 4: 334-365. [169]

RICHARDSON, L. F. (1960) Statistics of Deadly Quarrels. Pittsburgh and Chicago: Boxwood and Quadrangle. [97, 109, 110, 127, 129, 142, 174, 176]

――― (1952) "Contiguity and deadly quarrels: the local pacifying influence." J. of the Royal Statistical Society 115: 219-231. [148]

RIESELBACH, L. N. (1964) "The demography of the congressional vote on foreign aid, 1939-1958." Amer. Pol. Sci. Rev. 58: 577-588. [66, 67]

RITTBERGER, V. (1971) "Organized multinational cooperation within regional settings: a preliminary analysis." Peace Research Society Papers 17: 93-118. [113, 172, 173]

ROSECRANCE, R. N. (1963) Action and Reaction in World Politics. Boston: Little, Brown. [87-88]

ROSENAU, J. N. (1968) "Private preferences and political responsibilities: the relative potency of individual and role variables in the behavior of U.S. senators," pp. 17-50 in J. D. Singer (ed.) Quantitative International Politics. New York: Free Press. [62, 67, 223]

ROSI, E. J. (1965) "Mass and attentive opinion on nuclear weapons tests and fallout, 1954-1963." Public Opinion Q. 29: 280-297. [200-201]

RUBINSTEIN, A. Z. (1964) "Soviet and American policies in international economic organization." Internatl. Organization 18: 29-52. [85, 208-209]

RUGE, M. H. (1964) "Technical assistance and parliamentary debates." J. of Peace Research 1: 77-94. [125-126]

RUMMELL, R. J. (1972) The Dimensionality of Nations. Beverly Hills and London: Sage Publications. [36]

——— (1969) "Some empirical findings on nations and their behavior." World Politics 21: 226-241. [85, 98, 108, 111, 115, 118, 121, 127, 129-130, 134, 163, 173, 205, 206]

——— (1968) "The relationship Between national attributes and foreign conflict behavior," pp. 187-214 in J. D. Singer (ed.) Quantitative International Politics. New York: Free Press. [79, 95, 97, 109, 129, 134, 135]

——— (1967a) "Dimensions of dyadic war, 1820-1952." J. of Conflict Resolution 11: 176-183. [127, 176]

——— (1967b) "Some attributes and behavioral patterns of nations." J. of Peace Research 4: 196-206. [79-109]

——— (1966a) "A social field theory of foreign conflict behavior." Peace Research Society Papers 4: 131-150. [98]

——— (1966b) "Some dimensions in the foreign behavior of nations." J. of Peace Research 3: 201-224. [205]

——— (1964) "Testing some possible predictors of conflict within and between nations." Peace Research Society Papers 1: 79-111. [199]

——— (1963) "Dimensions of conflict behavior within and between nations." General Systems Yearbook 8: 1-50. [79, 204]

RUSSETT, B. M. (1968a) "Regional trading patterns, 1938-1963." Internatl. Studies Q. 12: 360-379. [177-178]

——— (1968b) "International communication and legislative behavior: the Senate and the House of Commons," pp. 81-102 in L. Kriesberg (ed.) Social Processes in International Relations. New York: John Wiley. [61]

——— (1967) International Regions and the International System. Chicago: Rand McNally. [44, 84, 97, 134, 139, 140, 167]

——— (1966) "Discovering voting groups in the United Nations." Amer. Pol. Sci. Rev. 60: 327-339. [84, 137, 168]

——— (1963) "The calculus of deterrence." J. of Conflict Resolution 7: 97-109. [99, 141]

——— and W. C. LAMB (1969) "Global patterns of diplomatic exchange, 1963-1964." J. of Peace Research 6: 37-55. [140, 170]

SALMORE, S. A. and C. F. HERMANN (1969) "The effect of size, development and accountability on foreign policy." Peace Research Society Papers 14: 15-30. [94, 98, 108, 118]

SCHMITT, B. E. (1961) "The relation of public opinion and foreign affairs before and during the First World War," pp. 322-330 in A. O. Sarkissian (ed.) Studies in Diplomatic History and Historiography. London: Longmans, Green. [78]

SCHWARTZ, D. C. (1967) "Decision theories and crisis behavior: an empirical study of nuclear deterrence in international political crises." Orbis 11: 459-490. [57, 59-60, 78, 99, 151, 183-184, 187]

SIGAL, L. V. (1970) "The 'rational policy' model and the Formosa Straits crises." Internatl. Studies Q. 14: 121-156. [57, 59, 126]

SINGER, J. D. (1972) "The 'correlates of war' project: interim report and rationale." World Politics 24: 243-270. [37, 95-6, 119, 121, 166-167, 209]

——— and M. SMALL (1969) "National alliance commitments and war involvement, 1815-1945," pp. 513-542 in J. N. Rosenau (ed.) International Politics and Foreign Policy. New York: Free Press. [141]

——— (1968) "Alliance aggregation and the onset of war, 1815-1945," pp. 247-286 in J. D. Singer (ed.) Quantitative International Politics. New York: Free Press. [164]

——— (1966) "Formal alliances 1815-1939: a quantitative description." J. of Peace Research 3: 1-32. [141, 142, 176-177]

SINGER, J. D. and M. WALLACE (1970) "Intergovernmental organization and the preservation of peace, 1816-1964: some bivariate relationships." Internatl. Organization 24: 520-547. [164, 209]

SINGER, M. R. and B. SENSENIG III (1963) "Elections within the United Nations: an experimental study utilizing statistical analysis." Internatl. Organization 17: 901-925. [112, 138, 152]

SILVERSON, R. M. (1970) "International conflict and perceptions of injury: the case of the Suez crisis." Internatl. Studies Q. 14: 157-165. [133-134, 151, 183]

SMALL, M. and J. D. SINGER (1970) "Patterns in international warfare, 1816-1965." Annals 391: 145-155. [95, 102, 192-193, 205]

——— (1969) "Formal alliances, 1816-1945: an extension of the basic data." J. of Peace Research 6: 257-282. [164]

SMOKER, P. (1969) "A time series analysis of Sino and Indian relations." J. of Conflict Resolution 13: 172-191. [192]

——— (1967) "Nation-state escalation and international integration." J. of Peace Research 4: 60-74. [171, 207]

——— (1965) "Trade, defense, and the Richardson theory of arms races: a seven-nation study." J. of Peace Research 2: 161-176. [85-86 171, 206, 207-208]

——— (1964a) "Fear in the arms race: a mathematical study." J. of Peace Research 1: 55-63. [151]

——— (1964b) "Sino-Indian relations: a study of trade, communication, and defense." J. of Peace Research 1: 65-76. [135]

——— (1963) "A pilot study of the present arms race." General Systems Yearbook 8: 61-76. [151]

STOESSINGER, J. B. (1970) The United Nations and the Super Powers: United States-Soviet Interaction at the United Nations. New York: Random House. [101, 208]

TANSKY, L. (1967) U.S. and U.S.S.R. Aid to Developing Countries: A Comparative Study of India, Turkey, and the U.A.R. New York: Praeger. [155-156, 187, 188]

TANTER, R. (1970) "Toward a theory of conflict behavior in Latin America," pp. 153-179 in Robert Cox (ed.) The Politics of International Organization. New York: Praeger. [157, 203]

––– (1966) "Dimensions of conflict behavior within and between nations." J. of Conflict Resolution 10: 41-64. [79, 82, 178, 199, 204]

TERRELL, L. M. (1972) "Patterns of international involvement and international violence." Internatl. Studies Q. 16: 167-186. [205]

––– (1971) "Societal stress, political instability, and levels of military effort." J. of Conflict Resolution 15: 329-346. [83]

THOMPSON, W. R. (1970) "The Arab sub-system and the feudal pattern of interaction, 1965." J. of Peace Research 7: 151-167. [169, 170]

TODD, J. E. (1971) "The 'law-making' behavior of states in the United Nations as a function of their location within formal world regions." Internatl. Studies Q. 15: 297-315. [84-85, 138]

TOUVAL, S. (1966) "Africa's frontiers: reaction to colonial legacy." Internatl. Affairs (London) 42; 641-654. [96, 110, 148, 190-191]

VELLUT, J. L. (1967) "Smaller states and the problem of war and peace," J. of Peace Research 4: 252-269. [102, 115, 148, 155, 187]

VINCENT, J. E. (1971) "Predicting voting patterns in the General Assembly." Amer. Pol. Sci. Rev. 65: 471-495. [73, 84, 100, 111, 121, 130, 137]

––– (1970) "An analysis of caucusing group activity at the United Nations." J. of Peace Research 7: 133-150. [112]

––– (1969) "The convergence of voting and attitude patterns at the United Nations." J. of Politics 31: 952-983. [168-169]

––– (1968) "National attributes as predictors of delegate attitudes at the United Nations." Amer. Pol. Sci. Rev. 62: 916-931. [112, 122, 168]

VITAL, D. (1971) The Survival of Small States: Studies in Small Power/Great Power Conflict. London: Oxford Univ. Press. [158, 175]

WALLACE, M. D. (1971) "Power, status, and international war." J. of Peace Research 8: 23-36. [165]

WALLENSTEEN, P. (1968) "Characteristics of economic sanctions." J. of Peace Research 5: 248-267. [143, 148, 156, 188]

WALTERS, R. S. (1970) American and Soviet Aid: A Comparative Analysis. Pittsburgh: Univ. Of Pittsburgh Press. [71-72, 73, 115, 155-156, 187-188, 189, 193]

WALTZ, K. N. (1967) Foreign Policy and Democratic Politics: The American and British Experience. Boston: Little, Brown. [93-94]

WEEDE, E. (1970) "Conflict behavior of nation-states." J. of Peace Research 7: 229-235. [79-80, 95, 96, 120, 135, 163, 204]

WEIGERT, K. M. and R. E. RIGGS (1969) "Africa and United Nations elections: an aggregate data analysis." Internatl. Organization 23: 1-19. [101, 112]

WEINSTEIN, F. B. (1972) "The uses of foreign policy in Indonesia: an approach to the analysis of foreign policy in the less developed countries." World Politics 24: 356-381. [54, 77]

WILKENFELD, J. (1971) "Domestic and foreign conflict behavior of nations," pp. 189-204 in W. D. Coplin and C. W. Kegley, Jr., (eds.) A Multi-Method Introduction to International Politics. Chicago: Markham. [81, 82, 199]

——— (1969) "Some further findings regarding the domestic and foreign conflict behavior of nations." J. of Peace Research 6: 147-156. [81, 82, 199]

WITTKOPF, E. R. (1971) "The distribution of foreign aid in comparative perspective: an empirical study of the flow of foreign economic assistance, 1961-1967." Ph.D. dissertation. Syracuse, N.Y.: Syracuse University. [140, 152, 187]

WOLF, C., Jr. (1967) United States Policy and the Third World: Problems and Analysis. Boston: Little, Brown. [157, 203]

——— (1965) "The political effects of military programs: some indications from Latin America." Orbis 8: 871-893. [157, 203]

WOLFERS, A. (1940) Britain and France Between Two Wars: Conflicting Strategies of Peace from Versailles to World War II. New York: Harcourt, Brace [148, 206]

WRIGHT, Q. (1965) "The escalation of international conflicts." J. of Conflict Resolution 9: 434-449. [99, 110, 126, 176]

——— (1964) A Study of War. Chicago: Univ. of Chicago Press. [70, 81, 83, 95, 98, 109, 119-120, 127-128, 129, 134, 135, 136, 141, 162, 163-164, 166, 174, 196, 203, 208, 209, 210]

YOUNG, O. R. (1968) "Intermediaries and interventionists: third parties in the Middle East crisis." Internatl. J. 23: 52-73. [175, 206, 208, 210]

ZANINOVITCH, M. G. (1962) "Pattern analysis of variables within the international system: the Sino-Soviet example." J. of Conflict Resolution 6: 253-268. [184]

ZARTMAN, I. W. (1965) "The politics of boundaries in North and West Africa." J. of Modern African Studies 3: 155-174. [83]

ZINNES, D. A. (1968) "The expression and perception of hostility in prewar crisis: 1914," pages 85-119 in J. D. Singer (ed.) Quantitative International Politics. New York: Free Press. [54-55]

――― (1966) "A comparison of hostile behavior of decision-makers in simulate and historical data." World Politics 18: 474-502. [54-55, 61, 133-134]

――― (1962) "Hostility in international decision-making." J. of conflict Resolution 6: 236-243. [55-56, 59]

――― R. C. NORTH, and H. E. KOCH, Jr. (1961) "Capability, threat, and the outbreak of war." pp. 469-482 in J. N. Rosenau (ed.) International Politics and Foreign Policy. New York: Free Press. [159]

――― and J. WILKENFELD (1971) "An analysis of foreign conflict behavior of nations," pp. 167-213 in W. F. Hanrieder (ed.) Comparative Foreign Policy: Theoretical Essays. New York: David McKay. [82-83, 204]

INDEX

Accountability:
    and conflict and cooperation, 98
    and foreign policy behavior, 94
    and interactions, 101-102
Africa, 80, 83, 89, 101, 108, 111, 112, 113, 115, 121, 122, 136, 137,
        140, 142, 152, 158, 176, 190, 191, 203, 206, 210-211
African Foreign Relations and International Conflict Analysis
        (AFRICA), 39
Alker, H. R., 225n
Alliances:
    and war and conflict, 136, 141-142, 164
    and others' support, 149
    and UN voting, 136-137
    establishment of, 144
    intra-alliance conflict, 177
Almond, G. A., 132n
Analysis, levels of, 221-222
Arab subsystem, 169, 170
Argentina, 122
Arms race, in Middle East, 58, 110
Arms race escalation:
    and fear factor, 151
    and others' support, 149
    as action and response, 151
    of neutrals, 174
Attitudes:
    and elite recruitment, 66
    and foreign policy behavior, 54
    of UN delegates, 112, 122
    See also Images; Perceptions; Hostility, perception of
Australia, 144, 149, 207
Austria-Hungary, 54, 59, 67
Axioms, 23
Azar, E. E., 38, 39, 51n